Breaking the Stalemate

The Case for Engaging the Iranian Opposition

Copyright © 2015 by Metis Analytics

All rights reserved. In accordance with the US Copyright act of 1976, the scanning, uploading, and electronic sharing of any part of this book without the permission of the publisher is unlawful piracy and theft of the author's intellectual property. If you would like to use material from the book (other than for review purposes), prior written permission must be obtained by contacting the publisher at info@zolabooks.com. Thank you for your support of the author's rights.

Cover Illustration by Amy Madden
Cover design by Shannon Coffey
Interior design by Amanda Atkins

Zola Books
242 W 38th St, 2nd Floor
New York, NY 10018
www.zolabooks.com

The Zola Books name and logo are trademarks of Zola Books.

The publisher is not responsible for websites (or their content) that are not owned by the publisher.

First print edition: March 2015

ISBN: 978-0-692-39937-8

Contents

Preface

Chess is the quintessentially Persian game. It is complex and canny, rewarding patience, anticipation, strategy. With the game pieces representing a monarch's court, each piece has a different role and different capabilities, creating manifold choices that must be well understood and thoughtfully weighed by the player. In German the game is known as *Schach*, reflecting its Persian history and derived from the word "Shah." Instead of "checkmate," one says "Schach matt," an approximation of *Shah maat* – the king is dead.[1]

A chessboard has 64 squares. A good player can anticipate multiple courses of future action and can visualize victory on the basis of a series of moves, each one seemingly insignificant and minor and some of them detrimental in the short run. A good strategy can involve accepting or indeed choreographing initial losses in the interest of later improved positioning and eventual triumph; to deliberately sacrifice some of your own players/pieces is a normal part of the game. A serious player has an elaborate mental index of famous past games and of the numerous strategies of legendary great players, as well as a strong memory

---

[1] There was originally no queen, women being considered irrelevant to the exercise of strategy and power, and the queen is believed to be an innovation from the Middle Ages in Europe, where real queens played significant political roles and wished to see themselves reflected in this popular new import. Converting the former vizier into a queen not only became the global standard, it also made the only female the most powerful piece on the board. This is described in a fascinating book by Marilyn Yalom, *Birth of the Chess Queen: A History*, Harper Collins 2004.

for moves that have failed. Definitely, it is not a game that just anyone can play – at least not well.

We are not advocating that U.S. strategy and diplomacy should seek to emulate the complexities of chess – that goes against our cultural grain and is unlikely to succeed. But we do need to consider what game our adversary is playing, with chess by no means being the most worrisome. Chess has an established history that can be studied, and it has rules, and it allows for a draw. Our worst adversaries are those who play by no rules, but who instead specialize in understanding the rules by which we play in order to evade, exploit or contravene them. This is asymmetric warfare and we are proving to be very bad at it, although we should have an aptitude for it given our country's history, its tradition of rebellion, and given the composition and values of our society – but that is a matter for a different book.

In this volume, we look at the contemporary U.S.–Iranian relationship and its challenges and opportunities. That review will invariably surface observations about U.S. diplomacy more generally, which unfortunately is or has become increasingly linear and inflexible even as global challenges would require the opposite. We make up our minds about an individual, group, country or approach as though we were forming teams and could adhere to our choice for the entire duration of the game. This caused us, for instance, to cling to Iraqi prime minister Nouri al-Maliki long past the moment when he was a constructive actor, and far into the time when he instead was actively fomenting the sectarian rifts that paved the way for ISIS and its fateful alliance with frustrated Iraqi Sunnis, who were tired of being oppressed by Baghdad and could see no other resolution.

Iran provides a sadly perfect illustration of the rigidity in our diplomatic culture. We determine a set of responses – already congratulating ourselves for having more than just one – and then we stick to them as though we were playing a game with a simple set of rules and an umpire to enforce them. For Iran, post-Shah, our slender repertoire was "negotiate" or "sanction." The Iranian side had a far broader spectrum in its dealings with us – which arguably it hardly needed, as instead it could make do with a good cop/bad cop routine (a seemingly more moderate president/a hard-liner) that kept us going in circles while the opponent not only held firm to a position and behavior that we were trying to affect, but also advanced, gradually but steadily, towards a goal of nuclear capabilities.

Preface

A basic tool in even a rudimentary diplomatic arsenal is to identify and make use of the adversary's domestic critics and rivals, today often subsumed under the term "opposition." If we want evidence for the inability of U.S. policy to operate in complex strategic environments, we need look no further than at its approach to opposition leaders and opposition movements. At times we decide to trust certain groups or individuals without having properly assessed their credibility and capabilities; this was the case in the run-up to the Iraq invasion, arguably a risky and monumental endeavor that would have deserved the utmost in prior verification and information. Sometimes we blithely assume that an "opposition" is automatically a good and democratic thing and that any wrinkles will sort themselves out; this was the case in Libya, where we supported an overthrow of a sitting government with only the haziest notions of what might follow and who exactly was behind this overthrow and without studying the (readily available) facts regarding the regional, ethnic and clan dynamics in that country. Sometimes we decide to be shrewd, with disastrous consequences. In Afghanistan in the 1980s, operating on the false assumption that the Soviet Union would inevitably prevail, we decided to arm and falsely portray as "freedom fighters" a murderous bunch of hoodlums who with our help and to our surprise emerged victorious – and subsequently devastated their country in a lengthy civil war concluding with a victory by the most anti-democratic force of them all, the Taliban, which proceeded to forge an alliance with Al Qaeda (leading to Afghanistan's use as the organization's base to attack us on 9-11). Even today we still struggle with multiple layers of consequences from that original mistake, not least the damage to the fabric of our society and values. Lesson not learned, in Syria we once again planned to arm, train and equip groups who almost certainly would have turned on us at the earliest opportunity, and about whom we knew far too little.

Just as unaccountably, in some high-stakes situations where we really need to advance our strategic interests, we ignore promising opposition groups altogether. As though we are playing a simple game, we set down a few conclusions at the start and then adhere to them blindly. In Prime Minister Maliki we had a hostile head of state who had been enthroned by us but had then turned out to have an agenda different from what we had hoped, and who was imperiling everything we had fought for in the Iraq intervention. Then there's the case of the Kurds.

The Kurds were modern and almost unbelievably pro-American. Their region was largely stable and was experiencing significant growth. As allowed by the Iraqi Constitution, they had their own regional government with a president, a prime minister, a parliament and ministries, and as such they were developing ties to neighboring countries and to the EU. They repeatedly warned their U.S. counterparts that Maliki's misrule was creating deep societal fault lines, that the Sunni Arabs were increasingly alienated, that the Iraqi army was dysfunctional, and that U.S. objectives in the country were in peril.

But the U.S. had a previously determined policy line, and we were sticking to it: namely, we support Baghdad, we support the unity of Iraq, anything we do has to go through Baghdad and any appearance of accepting the possibility of Kurdish independence must be avoided. What that meant: even as Turkey, Iran and the EU were courting or at least seriously engaging the Kurds, we chose to sideline and repeatedly rebuff a stable, rational, pro-American, significant regional player in the interest of maintaining the fiction of an intact, happy post-Saddam Iraq. And then the wakeup call came: ISIS advanced on Mosul, the Sunni tribes collaborated with them, the Iraqi army turned and ran – exactly the picture the Kurds had been painting. The Kurdish armed force, the Peshmerga, held their ground somewhat, except that Baghdad had systematically deprived them of weapons and training and salaries to the point where they weren't in great fighting form either.

It's fine to have rules and an established policy, but those are not ends in themselves. What is the desired outcome? When circumstances change, policy may have to be reevaluated, and a crisis or a setback should be scrutinized for possible opportunities. Generally, this is not how U.S. foreign policy operates. Once formulated, it tends to be rigid and reactive, and nowhere is this more evident than in our relations with Iran.

Introduction

The Iranian Revolution in 1979 caught the United States by surprise. In short order, the United States went from having a staunch ally in the Middle East to suddenly being faced with a theocratic, anti-American regime that it did not understand.

Since then, the United States has struggled to find a coherent and effective approach towards Iran. U.S.-Iranian relations have gone through many different phases during which the United States has tried a variety of approaches, principally representing permutations of outreach, diplomacy, concessions and incentives on the one hand, and the imposition of sanctions and issuing of threats on the other.

More than three decades later, none of these approaches has yet borne fruit. Iran remains an anti-American theocracy oppressive to its citizenry and disruptive to world stability. On the face of it, the Iranian regime seems fairly resilient despite strong sanctions that have hurt the economy and despite significant, and by all accounts growing, fissures within the Iranian leadership and within Iranian society. The country is now very close to achieving a nuclear weapons capability. And through terrorist proxies like Hezbollah, and its role in agitating sectarian conflict, it poses a threat to U.S. interests in the Middle East and to regional and global stability.

The recent elections in Iran, which resulted in Hassan Rouhani becoming the country's new president, upon first evaluation appear to fit into the long-standing pattern of Iranian politics. Typically a hard-liner will serve as president for a time, and will advance a defiant set of policies around nuclear issues, support for groups like Hezbollah, and restrictions on the basic liberties of the Iranian people. International pressure will begin to mount, including sanctions and rhetoric around considering regime change. Then, just when it seems that international opinion has turned decidedly against the regime, the Ayatollahs orchestrate the election of a new, apparently more moderate president who creates hope that relations with the Iranian regime could develop in a new direction after all, and could slowly normalize. In the past, the moderate president has repeatedly turned out not to be such a moderate after all, or it turned out that the Supreme Leader and the Ayatollahs would not actually give the moderate president enough breathing room to enact genuine reforms.

Because the West prefers to avoid a confrontation with Iran, it inevitably overestimates the opportunity for accommodation every time a new, seemingly more moderate Iranian leader takes charge – thereby unwittingly accommodating Iran's strategy of cooling down the tensions between Iran and the West whenever Iran feels that actual repercussions may be imminent.

When Rafsanjani took office, for example, he was heralded as "the leader of Iran's pragmatists." Western commentators saw Rafsanjani's election as evidence that Iran's more radical forces were "on the wane [as] the revolution's repressive aspects are being relaxed, and ideology appears to be getting less attention."[1] Similarly, when Khatami was elected president, his victory was described as a demonstration of the "disillusionment with the ruling establishment...[and] an opportunity to break with the rigidity of the past and to put relations on a new, non-hostile footing."[2]

Today the commentariat is holding fast to its excitement over the potential to restart U.S.-Iranian relations with the help of President Rouhani. His election has been described as "heralding a new chapter in ties between Iran and the

---

[1] Judith Miller, "After the War: Islamic Radicals Lose Their Tight Grip on Iran," *New York Times*, April 8, 1991 <http://www.nytimes.com/1991/04/08/world/after-the-war-islamic-radicals-lose-their-tight-grip-on iran.html?ref=aliakbarhashemirafsanjani>

[2] Patrick Clawson, et al. "Iran Under Khatami: A Political, Economic, and Military Assessment," The Washington Institute for Near East Policy, October 1998 <http://www.washingtoninstitute.org/policy-analysis/view/iran-under-khatami-a-political-economic-and-military-assessment>

West,"[3] and as providing "latitude for a diplomatic thaw with the West and more social freedoms at home."[4]

A sea change in Iranian politics towards a greater willingness to reasonable negotiation, if real, would be welcome, and one can understand the inclination of some Western analysts and politicians to hope that Rouhani represents such a change. And of course it is possible that the revolutionary zeal of Iranian hard-liners has been eroded by decades of global marginalization, that pragmatic interests and the public will are beginning to assert themselves in a real way, that a critical mass of decision-makers is ready to make genuine compromises in order for Iran to reassume its place as a respected international player. This would be positive and would deserve encouragement and a parallel willingness to explore and engage. Indeed, this outcome is sufficiently desirable that Western diplomacy should go beyond a reactive stance and should consider what additional pressure points it can bring to bear, what additional actors it can place on the stage, to better shape the desired result. As we have concluded and will explain in the sections that follow, this includes a far more engaged and nuanced relationship with Iranian opposition forces.

Rouhani's election does have the hallmarks of another calibrated attempt by Iran to dial down the level of tension between Iran and the West, à la Rafsanjani or Khatami – only this time, with Iran even closer to achieving nuclear capability, the stakes are even higher and the window in which to experiment with possible rapprochement is even narrower. Rouhani's biography, as well, gives little cause for optimism, offering no reason to classify him either as a social reformer or as someone willing to compromise on Iran's nuclear ambitions. He has been a core member of the dominant elite and considered more reliable than Rafsanjani, who was not permitted to run for office. He was Khamenei's representative in the Supreme National Security Council and a member of the Assembly of Experts and the Expediency Council. Rather alarmingly, he is on record bragging about his ability to deceive the West in nuclear negotiations, in

---

[3] Jason Rezaian and Joby Warrick, "Moderate Cleric Hassan Rouhani Wins Iran's Presidential Vote," *Washington Post*, June 15, 2013 <http://articles.washingtonpost.com/2013-06-15/world/39983644_1_iranians-vote-final-results>

[4] Zahra Hosseinian, "Iran's New President Hails 'Victory of Moderation,'" *Reuters*, June 15, 2013

which he previously held a leading role.[5] He has publicly defended the suppression of regime critics and Iran's support of Assad in Syria. He has signaled his strong support of Hezbollah and desire to confront Israel.[6] And his record as a high-ranking member of the regime for three decades holds no indication that he intends to, or could, chart an independent course.

Indeed, in a recent speech, Ayatollah Khamenei made it quite clear that chances for a genuine rapprochement between the United States and Iran are slim:

> Achieving improved political relations with the U.S. is against our interest. First, this does not reduce the U.S. threat against Iran. The U.S. attacked Iraq while it had political relations with the country, they had mutual ambassadors. Having diplomatic relations does not obviate the threat. Secondly, having diplomatic relations for America has always been an opportunity to recruit mercenaries. The British were the same. For years, their embassy was the point of contact with individuals who were prepared to sell themselves to the enemy. This is one of the tasks of the embassies. The U.S. embassy was the heart and center of all the riots and disturbances, which happened about 17 or 18 years ago in China, and the huge publicity it created. But, in Iran, they confront a vacuum. They need to have a base, but they do not have one. Now, some among us argue that not having diplomatic relations with the U.S. is against our interest. But actually, this is beneficial for us.[7]

Most disturbing and disappointing, however, is the human rights record

---

[5] In a *Sunday Telegraph* article under the heading of "How we duped the West, by Iran's nuclear negotiator," Philip Sherwell wrote on March 5, 2006: "The man who for two years led Iran's nuclear negotiations has laid out in unprecedented detail how the regime took advantage of talks with Britain, France and Germany to forge ahead with its secret atomic program. In a speech to a closed meeting of leading Islamic clerics and academics, Hassan Rouhani, who headed talks with the so-called EU3 until last year, revealed how Teheran played for time and tried to dupe the West after its secret nuclear program was uncovered by the Iranian opposition in 2002."

[6] "New Iran president backs Syria's Assad, Hezbollah," *Associated Press*, July 16, 2014 <http://news.yahoo.com/iran-president-backs-syrias-assad-hezbollah-132644190.html>

[7] See response by Ayatollah Khamenei reported by Fars News Agency, March 3, 2013 <http://www.farsnews.com/newstext.php?nn=13911212000249>

under Rouhani. Improvements and reforms had been anticipated; instead, the U.N. Rapporteur found that abuses had significantly worsened under his governance. According to the "Situation of Human Rights in the Islamic Republic of Iran," published in August 2014[8], executions on arbitrary grounds (including executions of juveniles) increased, the right to expression and association was further undermined, the legal status of women was additionally eroded, and minorities were increasingly suppressed. The report noted "an alarming increase in the number of executions in relation to the already-high rates of previous years" and a steady stream of legal initiatives intended to sharpen rather than soften the restrictions on any form of free expression and critique. Domestically, this is no reformer and arguably no moderate.

Elsewhere, the U.S. at times takes a stringent view of foreign rulers' domestic policies. Perhaps in the case of Iran, for a range of good reasons, the decision was made to ignore the country's domestic circumstances. Even then, though, from a U.S. policy perspective, it must be concluded that more than 30 years of different strategies – and dealing repeatedly with both "moderate" Iranian presidents and hard-line Iranian presidents – have failed to put in place a working relationship with the Iranian government, and that what has endured instead is a government which is unwilling to assume a responsible role in the global scene, and that continues to engage in significant and ongoing support of terrorism and fostering of sectarian strife.

Neither softball nor hardball may suffice here; we may need to up our game by bringing in a new player: the Iranian opposition.

Experts at times express the view that there is no Iranian opposition worth talking about, but this depends on your definition. If by opposition we mean armed groups in the manner of Libya or Syria, then no, Iran does not have such – a circumstance difficult to regret, given how things are unfolding in those two countries. If by opposition we mean an ongoing, intellectually robust critique of an authoritarian system with ties to popular sentiment, one including persons who are willing to take significant risks and losses for their beliefs – in the manner of Cold War dissidents – and to hold to those beliefs for decades with little encouragement by the outside world, then Iran has a rather impressive

---

[8] United Nations, General Assembly, August 27, 2014, A/69/356. <http://shaheedoniran.org/wp-content/uploads/2014/09/A-69-356-SR-Report-Iran.pdf>

opposition. It seems obvious that it would, at the very least, make sense to seek to understand this opposition better: its size, composition, internal relationships and rifts, goals and abilities, as well as to estimate the potential it might unfold if indeed it did receive advice and various levels and types of support.

At present, U.S. government officials are not even allowed to have meetings with members of the Iranian opposition as part of President Obama's strategy of offering olive branches to the Iranian government in the hopes that these olive branches might coax Iran to come to a negotiated agreement regarding its nuclear program.

It is our contention, however, that the Iranian opposition contributes an important additional set of options that can, if properly developed, increase the chance of a positive outcome under the entire spectrum of likely scenarios:

- If the Iranian regime is not actually thinking of true engagement and compromise, but is merely continuing the familiar pattern of seductive advances to obtain a tactical gain, followed by a return to hostile rigidity, then upon the next cycle of this fruitless exercise, it may be time to think of regime change.

- The fact that the West has other potential political partners in Iran, and a coherent strategy for advancing the abilities of those partners, is likely to enhance the willingness of the regime to compromise, if elements within are truly able to do this and are so inclined.

- If the regime is sincere in its current outreach, then the political moderation in its foreign policy and nuclear aims will need to be accompanied also by improvements in the domestic political domain in the direction of more civil rights and greater democratic freedoms. A strengthened and prepared opposition can step into whatever political space is thereby opened, and ensure that the opportunity is adequately and calmly utilized.

- Assuming the most positive outcome, that the process is sincere and goes forward and results in an open society in Iran, developing the opposition now will ensure a smoother transition to democracy and will potentially avoid some of the problems experienced by other countries where democratic institutions and rules of engagement were not in place, such as post-Saddam Iraq.

There is an additional possibility that deserves consideration. It is conceivable that the Iranian regime, far from acting out of exhaustion or as a consequence of internal rifts or because the sanctions have been so debilitating, in fact considers itself to be acting from a position of strength. They may feel that they have essentially "won," that they have achieved or are on the verge of achieving their principal aims and are therefore ready to reclaim their place in the international system — after having de facto forced that system to accept and come to terms with its protracted violation of the rules. If this is the case, and particularly in light of the current situation in the region, we must add one more contingency:

- If Iran believes that it has once more successfully played the 'stall, delay and continue to build' game in its nuclear negotiations (gaining additional time without having given up anything of significance), and additionally can now portray itself as a valuable partner in solving the IS crisis in Syria and Iraq, then the U.S. should seek to obtain at least some degree of leverage by moving into the Iranian domestic equation via the opposition, in order to obtain a somewhat better outcome in terms of a reasonable counterpart whose foreign policy goals are slightly more aligned with U.S. interests.

It is important to fully explore and give every chance to the possibility that a diplomatic breakthrough with Iran is today possible: that the exhaustion wrought by the sanctions, combined with the unique personality of Rouhani, the estrangement among hard-liner Iranian inner circles and a far more liberal public are culminating in a moment where serious dialogue can take place.

However, it is equally important to plan for the possibility that this will turn out to have been, as in the past, an overly optimistic assessment either because Iran never intended to follow through, or was unable to go far enough, for its own internal reasons. Under that circumstance, the West cannot afford to be left dumbstruck and with no alternative policy. That, however, is a very real risk. Before this most recent election, recall that U.S. experts were broadly bemoaning a situation in which the U.S. was "out of options" because the sanctions had gone as far as they could, efforts at negotiation were consistently thwarted, agreements were circumvented or ignored, a strike against nuclear facilities was too difficult and a military intervention too risky. If current hopes are not fulfilled, this is exactly where we will be once again, except that Iran will be that many months closer to achieving its nuclear ambitions.[9]

In considering its policy options, the U.S. analytic community has tended to be reactive, waiting to see what posture Tehran was taking and then attempting to either counter or encourage that posture. On the proactive side, little was put forward except for the two extremes: to make unilateral gestures of reconciliation and hope this would inspire an equivalent response, or to ratchet up the punitive measures, from strong sanctions all the way to threats of military action. What often seemed to go overlooked was that the U.S. had additional courses of action, that there were a host of sophisticated and asymmetrical approaches through which the United States could begin to mobilize its significant resources in favor of influencing or if necessary changing the Iranian regime.

Principal among these neglected avenues of influence is the Iranian opposition. Both inside Iran and among Iran's large, well-educated, well-resourced, and well-connected Diaspora community, multiple groups, influential individuals, and cliques of activists have formed or regrouped. They have different ideologies and different agendas. Some are pro-American and some are not; some have meaningful capabilities and some less so. In other words, not all of them offer value to U.S. foreign policy. Some would, though, and a policy of providing better support for those helpful elements of the Iranian opposition may offer opportunities for encouraging a better outcome during the current period of mutual testing and attempted dialogue, or of accelerating the ultimate demise of the Iranian regime and its replacement with a more responsible and more contemporary government if this fails.

Currently, the United States does not have a very strong understanding of who the opposition groups are and what role they might play for the betterment

---

[9]For a detailed review of possible negative outcomes of a military intervention, see Austin Long, William Luers, "Weighing Benefits and Costs of Military Action Against Iran," The Iran Project, The Wilson Center: New York, 2012. Executive Summary at http://thinkprogress.org/wp-content/uploads/2012/09/IranReport_091112_ExecutiveSummary.pdf

of their country. Policymakers and analysts have assumptions and stereotypes about the various opposition groups, but actual data and information are surprisingly scarce given the amount of time that has passed, the importance of Iran to U.S. policy, and the comparative accessibility of information resources.

This report steps into that gap. It analyzes the Iranian opposition, describing the various groups from the standpoint of their ideologies and their capabilities. It concludes by offering recommendations for how the United States can more effectively work with the Iranian opposition to achieve our common foreign policy objectives. A fresh look at U.S. policy options is critical at this juncture. If indeed there is a sea change in U.S.-Iranian relations, it will be essential to maximize that opportunity and ensure that the Iranian political process can be populated with a range of genuine choices and responsible leaders. Libya, Syria, and Egypt illustrate the dangers of conducting foreign policy and encouraging political transformations while knowing too little about the actors in play and those waiting in the wings. In Iran, Western policymakers still have an opportunity to understand the setting and to get to know the likely future players before they enter the stage. Conversely, if the renewed effort at negotiating fails, then considering Iran's progress on its nuclear program, time will basically have run out for the West and there may be no alternative to regime change before the chaos erupts. Arguably, such a change will be better if effected by internal forces than by a military intervention.

PART I

Background

1. Iran Today

Iran today is a country facing substantial domestic and international pressures – as well as a country that is causing considerable strain to global stability, U.S. foreign policy goals, and the well-being of its own population. Domestically, Iran is plagued by a weak economy and widespread disaffection with the regime as well as various political fissures within the regime itself. Internationally, Iran has increasingly become a pariah as its refusal to abandon its nuclear ambitions has resulted in strong condemnation and a sanctions regime that has grown more robust over the years and that has been a substantial factor in the weakening of Iran's economy.

At the same time, however, Iran has shown tremendous resilience, and its rulers have proven adept at managing and, in many cases, outwitting external efforts to change their behavior and policies. Despite the lack of freedoms and the economic hardships that average Iranians endure on a daily basis, the core institutions of the Iranian regime appear to be holding up. The political shake-ups that occurred throughout the Middle East over the course of the Arab Spring did not spread to Iran. The country's population, though disaffected, appears less prepared to contest the regime today, having suffered grave consequences for taking to the streets in 2009. However, some suggest that the fire is still smoldering under the ashes. Given the history of Iran, this notion cannot simply be rejected as wishful thinking. Nobody predicted the 2009 uprising or the 1979 revolution.

1.1: The Iranian Political System: A Theocracy with Multiple Power Centers

To understand the current state of Iran, it is important to review the structure of the Iranian political system.

The Constitution of the Islamic Republic of Iran, which governs the country to this day, was drafted by a body of Khomeinist clerics, the Assembly of Experts ("*majlis-e-khobregan*"), endorsed through a popular referendum in November 1979, and amended in 1989. This constitution sets up a complex structure with some elected elements, but in practice, Iran is a theocracy in which real power lies with the Supreme Leader, the Council of Guardians, the Revolutionary Guards, and the security services.

The concept of "Guardianship of the Jurist" ("*velayat-e faqih*") endows the Supreme Leader with vast powers as the ultimate political and religious authority in Iran. While this concept, promulgated by Khomeini, had little basis in Shi'ite political thinking, Khomeini argued that rather than waiting for the prophesized arrival of the "hidden Imam," other qualified clerics ought to serve as interim stewards of the government. The selection of the Supreme Leader was given to the Assembly of Experts. Under the Constitution, the Supreme Leader is the commander in chief of all armed forces and alone has the capacity to appoint and dismiss commanders, mobilize troops, and declare war. He can dismiss and appoint the heads of the judiciary, the heads of state radio and television, as well as the president if either the judiciary or the parliament decides that the president should be removed for cause.[1]

The president is the nominal head of government with the authority to dismiss and appoint ministers, who must also be confirmed by parliament. The president also controls the Planning and Budget Organization, which does pro-

---

[1] See Vanessa Martin, *Creating an Islamic State: Khomeini and the Making of a New Iran*, London: I.B. Taurus, 2000; Wilfried Buchta, *Who Rules Iran? The Structure of Power in the Islamic Republic*, Washington Institute for Near East Policy, 2002; Robin Wright, ed., *The Iran Primer: Power, Politics, and U.S. Policy*, U.S. Institute of Peace, 2010; Kenneth Katzman, "Iran: U.S. Concerns and Policy Responses," Congressional Research Service, September 5, 2012.

vide the president with considerable influence over economic policy. The president also appoints the head of the Central Bank and the chairs of the National Security Council. The president can be removed if there is a two-thirds majority no-confidence vote in the parliament; his ministers can be removed by a simple majority vote. Article 110 of the constitution also empowers the parliament to declare the president "politically incompetent." Upon being informed of this judgment, the Supreme Leader is permitted to remove the president from office.

In theory, the president is the second most powerful person in the Iranian political system, but he does not in fact control any of the military and security organs. He chairs the National Security Council, but military and security affairs fall within the purview of the Supreme Leader and are controlled by him and close allies. In actuality, the Iranian presidency has little control over internal security and foreign policy. The presidency is beholden to the Supreme Leader for its authority and is only as powerful as the Supreme leader allows it to be. As president, Mahmoud Ahmadinejad tried unsuccessfully to expand the powers of the president vis-à-vis the Supreme Leader. Ahmadinejad was powerless to change his own Minister of Intelligence, Heydar Moslehi, whom he attempted to dismiss but whom the Supreme Leader supported and kept in the role. In a speech in October 2011, as his feud with Ahmadinejad escalated, Supreme Leader Ali Khamenei even raised the possibility of abolishing the position of president.[2] President Rouhani will be severely constrained in his ability to chart a more moderate course for Iran, even if we assume that he desires to pursue a reformist policy agenda, which is a major question given his intimate and long-standing ties to the regime.

The Council of Guardians, currently headed by Ayatollah Ahmad Jannati, is comprised of twelve members appointed for six-year terms. Six members are clerics appointed by the Supreme Leader and six are jurists appointed by the judiciary and confirmed by the parliament. The Council determines whether or not legislation passed by the parliament is consistent with Islamic law and screens candidates for elected office. Thus, it is the Guardian Council and not Iran's Supreme Court or its head of the judiciary that holds the power of interpreting the constitution and the right of judicial review. It is well known that the

---

[2] See "Iran's Politics: President v Supreme Leader," *The Economist*, November 5, 2011 <http://www.economist.com/node/21536660>

Council of Guardians is a bastion of conservatives.[3]

The Expediency Council is endowed with two responsibilities: resolving conflicts between the parliament and the Council of Guardians and advising the Supreme Leader. The members of the Expediency Council are appointed by the Supreme Leader for five-year terms. This body has played an influential role at various times. In 1997, under the chairmanship of Ali Akbar Hashemi Rafsanjani, the Council checked some of President Mohammad Khatami's reformist initiatives. In 2006, the powers of the Council were expanded to include oversight of the executive branch's performance. Rafsanjani was reappointed as chairman in 2012 despite his perceived disloyalty to the Supreme Leader during the 2009 presidential election.[4] In practice, the Expediency Council has gradually become less influential and currently does not play a major role in policy-making in the Islamic Republic; however, it continues to be a power base for Rafsanjani. More recently, Khamenei also appointed Ahmadinejad as a member of the Expediency Council.

The Assembly of Experts is essentially a tool of the Supreme Leader in the guise of an elected, democratic institution. The Assembly is a council of 86 clerics who are popularly elected for eight-year terms. As with all electoral proceedings, candidates are pre-approved by the Council of Guardians. In this way, Iran's power centers can control the process, barring candidates who are not deemed suitable or who could pose too much of a challenge to the system.

The primary task of the Assembly of Experts is to appoint the Supreme Leader upon the death of the incumbent and, since 1989, to remove him should they find that he is unable or unwilling to execute his duties or if he is deemed to be unqualified to hold the office.[5]

The parliament ("*Majlis*") is elected every four years. It is responsible for drafting legislation, approving states of emergency, ratifying treaties, approving loans and annual budget, and dismissing the president and his ministers. Howev-

---

[3] See Pierre Tristam, "What Is Iran's Council of Guardians?" *Middle East Issues* <http://middleeast.about.com/od/iran/f/council-of-guardians.htm>

[4] See Kenneth Katzman, "Iran: U.S. Concerns and Policy Responses," Congressional Research Service, September 5, 2012, p. 3-4.

[5] See Pierre Tristam, "What Is Iran's Assembly of Experts?" *Middle East Issues* <http://middleeast.about.com/od/iran/f/assembly-of-experts.htm>; Katzman, "U.S. Concerns and Policy Responses," p. 8-9.

er, in practice, the actual authority of this institution is heavily circumscribed by non-elected centers of power.

As noted, there are several bodies charged with some form of internal security such as the Islamic Revolutionary Guards Corps ("IRGC"), the Basij, the Ministry of Intelligence and Security, and the Special Court. The IRGC runs a parallel military and intelligence establishment and conducts covert operations abroad in coordination with Iranian proxies and allied groups. The IRGC has also gained control over important sectors of the Iranian economy. It is closely associated with hard-line conservative elements in the government. The Basij militia is recruited from among poorly educated and deeply religious young people from rural areas or impoverished urban areas. Basijis are used as shock troops to suppress dissent or unrest. The Ministry of Intelligence and Security is the largest and most powerful intelligence agency in Iran. It is notorious for repressive and coercive methods. The Special Clerical Court has no legal basis in the constitution and is responsible only to the Supreme Leader. Its main function is to handle alleged conspiracies against or defamation of the Supreme Leader. For instance, Ayatollah Mohammad Kazem Shariatmadari, an early critic of Khomeini's theory of *velayat-e faqih* and a respected, prominent cleric, was "tried" by this court. Many of his relatives and followers were arrested or executed and he was shown on television making a "confession."[6]

Iran's governing system, then, is heavily dominated by the Supreme Leader and by various organs that he directly or indirectly appoints and controls. This helps to explain why many presidents who over the years were heralded as potential reformists or as leaders who could significantly change the dynamics between Iran and the United States have repeatedly failed to live up to these expectations.

1.2: Iranian Society

Iran's population suffers under the heavy hand of its government, which strives to control all aspects of daily life. Certain segments of society, especially women, youth, and ethno-religious minorities, face the most intrusive and consistent abuse by authorities. Many Iranians harbor deep resentment against the government for the state of affairs and respond through political activism; others react with apathy or various kinds of escapism because they feel powerless to catalyze meaningful change. This section focuses on Iran's youth. Section 1.5 below will explore the

---

[6] See Medhi Khalaji, "The Iranian Clergy's Silence," *Current Trends in Islamist Ideology*, Vol. 10, July 12, 2010 <http://www.currenttrends.org/research/detail/the-iranian-clergys-silence>

plight of Iran's women and minorities in the context of the regime's oppressive domestic policies.

Over 60% of Iran's population is under the age of thirty. Its youth are politically active and arguably the most restive part of its society. University students and other young activists formed the core of the 2009 uprisings (as discussed below) and drive other political reform efforts. Other segments of Iran's youth, however, are extremely apathetic and prone to drug use to escape from the daily realities of their lives. In addition to the political, economic, and other challenges facing all Iranians, four issues are particularly acute for Iran's youth: unemployment, lack of independence, sexual conduct, and drug abuse.[7]

Iran's economic woes (discussed below in Section 1.3) have disproportionately affected the young. There is a severe shortage of jobs, even for university graduates: youth unemployment is estimated at upwards of 40%[8] and chronic underemployment is common, too. In July 2013, President Rouhani expressed concern about the poor job prospects of educated young people and estimated that Iran "will have 4.5 million unemployed university graduates" in four years' time.[9]

Poor job prospects coupled with increasing housing costs have contributed to the increasing number of young Iranians who remain dependent on their parents through their late 20s. This lack of independence engenders pessimism about the future and deep frustration with Iran's government.[10] These factors have also contributed to "brain drain" in Iran, which occurs at the highest rate of any country worldwide according to the IMF.[11]

Iran's youth also faces a sexual revolution in part because social interaction between unmarried men and women is prohibited and subject to severe punishment.[12] Pardis Mahdavi, an Associate Professor of Anthropology at Pomona

---

[7] See Omid Memarian and Tara Nesvaderani, "The Iran Primer: The Youth," United States Institute of Peace, <http://iranprimer.usip.org/resource/youth>

[8] See "Iranian Youth Struggle with Unemployment," Al Jazeera, June 13, 2013 <http://www.aljazeera.com/video/middleeast/2013/06/20136136295061524.html>

[9] See Thomas Erdrink and Rick Gladstone, "Iran's Next President Faults Ahmadinejad on Economy," New York Times, July 15, 2013 <http://www.nytimes.com/2013/07/16/world/middleeast/irans-president-elect-describes-a-bleak-economy.html?ref=global-home>

[10] See Memarian and Nesvaderani, "The Iran Primer: The Youth"

[11] See "Iran's Exiles Lament Brain Drain and Miss Home, but Offer Those Trapped Behind a Voice, Euronews, June 9, 2013 <http://www.euronews.com/2013/06/09/iran-s-exiles-lament-brain-drain-and-miss-home-but-offer-those-trapped-behind-a/>

[12] See Memarian and Nesvaderani, "The Iran Primer: The Youth"

College, who has studied the interplay between sexuality and politics post-Revolution, stresses that "in the absence of any option for overt political dissent... [s]ex has become both a source of freedom and an act of political rebellion."[13] The regime has responded to this crisis by promoting temporary marriages, which can be as brief as a few hours or days and which are recognized by some Shi'ite clerics.[14] There is growing concern within the UN and international health circles that unconsidered sexual behavior by Iran's youth is promoting the spread of HIV/AIDS, which is concentrated in the country's 25-to-34 year-old age group.[15]

Drug abuse is a grave problem in Iran and is concentrated amongst its youth and women.[16] The country seizes more opium and heroin annually than any other country in the world.[17] Iran also has one of the world's most serious opiate addiction problems, with an estimated over 1.2 million addicts (or 2.26% of the population).[18] Accurate data is hard to come by, and some reports estimate the number of drug addicts at 2 million or nearly 4% of its population.[19] HIV is spread by drug use and is particularly high among needle-sharing drug users.[20]

1.3: Iran's Economy

Obtaining reliable data on Iran's economy is difficult because official figures are manipulated to hide the stagnation of the formal economy and concomitant expansion of the informal economy. According to the IMF, Iran's economy shrank by an estimated 1.4% in 2012 and was projected to contract further in

---

[13] See Pardis Mahdavi, *Passionate Uprisings: Iran's Sexual Revolution*, Stanford University Press, 2009.

[14] See Memarian and Nesvaderani, "The Iran Primer: The Youth"

[15] See "The Prevention and Control of HIV/AIDS in Iran," United Nations Development Programme, February 27, 2011 <http://www.undp.org.ir/index.php/millennium-development-goals/481-27-february-2011-the-prevention-and-control-of-hivaids-in-iran>

[16] See "Technical Cooperation on Drugs and Crime in the Islamic Republic of Iran 2011-2014," United Nations Office on Drugs and Crime, June 2011 <http://www.unodc.org/documents/islamicrepublicofiran//CP_Iran11-14.pdf>

[17] See "Drug Trafficking and Border Control Situation Analysis," United Nations Office on Drugs and Crime, Accessed June 16, 2013 <http://www.unodc.org/islamicrepublicofiran/drug-trafficking-and-border-control.html>

[18] See "Technical Cooperation on Drugs and Crime in the Islamic Republic of Iran"

[19] See Christian Oliver, "Iran Opium Addicts Find Supplies Despite Earthquake," *Reuters*, January 3, 2004. http://www.opioids.com/opium/iran.html

[20] See "Technical Cooperation on Drugs and Crime in the Islamic Republic of Iran"

2013.[21] Multiple indicators illustrate the extent of Iran's economic malaise, but experts disagree over its primary cause. Many argue that U.S. and EU sanctions have crippled Iran's oil and gas industry and financial sector, thereby depriving the country of much-needed oil revenue and hard currency. Others point to Iranian government interference, corruption, and economic mismanagement as the root causes of Iran's weak economy. A rigorous econometric analysis that compares Iran to other similarly-situated countries concludes that sanctions have "adversely affected the Iranian economy."[22] In remarks to the *Majlis* in July 2013, President Rouhani laid much of the blame for Iran's bleak economy on the outgoing Ahmadinejad government's failed policies.[23]

While the picture is mixed and the country has devised ways to deal with the effect of the sanctions, two conclusions are inescapable. Overall, Iran's citizens are suffering the effects of its poor economy. And the sanctions have been effective, especially over time, and represent a significant impairment to the regime's ability to operate.

Iran's economy is highly dependent on oil. Crude exports traditionally constituted 80% of its hard currency earnings and 50% of its government revenue.[24] Oil production dropped precipitously in 2012 to fewer than 3 million barrels, most likely due to sanctions and aging infrastructure. Exports dropped some 40% from an average of 2.5 million bpd to less than 1.4 million bpd during the same period.[25] Tehran's oil minister publically confirmed the large decrease in Iran's oil sales (40% in 2012) and repatriated oil earnings (45% in 2012).[26] Experts estimate that Iran lost up to $40 billion in revenue as a result.[27] This in turn contributed to Iran running in 2012 its largest budget deficit since 1998, which

---

[21] See United States Government Accountability Office, *U.S. and International Sanctions Have Adversely Affected the Iranian Economy*, February 2013 (GAO-13-326) p. 32. [GAO Report]
[22] See GAO Report, p. 27.
[23] See Erdink and Gladstone "Iran's Next President Faults Ahmadinejad on Economy"
[24] See Kenneth Katzman, "Iran Sanctions," Congressional Research Service, July 26, 2013, p. 54
[25] See "Iran Crude oil exports rise to highest since EU sanctions," *Reuters*, January 30, 2013 <http://www.reuters.com/article/2013/01/31/us-iran-oil-exports-idUSBRE90U01Y20130131>
[26] See Rick Gladstone, "Iran Oil Minister Concedes Sanctions Have Hurt Exports," *New York Times*, January 7, 2013 < http://www.nytimes.com/2013/01/08/world/middleeast/irans-oil-exports-and-sales-down-40-percent-official-admits.html?_r=0>
[27] See "Despite Being Economically Unfree, Iran's Economy Shows Resilience," *Forbes*, April 5, 2013.

totaled an estimated 3% of GDP.[28] Some sources allege that the government has also dangerously leveraged itself within Iran, owing some $387 billion, nearly twice the annual budget of Iran, to local banks and individuals.[29] As of July 2013, Iran was more than six months overdue on $81 million dollars of loans it owed the World Bank; Zimbabwe is the only other country on the World Bank's non-performing list.[30]

Iran also faces ever-increasing inflation. On April 1, 2013, the Iranian government announced that inflation had exceeded 40% in the previous twelve-month period, verging on hyperinflation.[31] President Rouhani told the *Majlis* in July 2013 that official inflation figures underestimate actual inflation, which is above 40%.[32] The rial, Iran's currency, lost nearly 70% of its value against the U.S. dollar between 2010 and 2012.[33] The outgoing Ahmadinejad regime cut the official exchange rate in half in June 2013 from 12,260 to 24,500 rials to the dollar (even though the true value as of August was over 30,000).[34]

The decline sparked protests in Tehran in late 2012, including in the traditionally pro-Khamenei bazaar, as Iranian purchasing power plummeted and the price of staple food items soared.[35] Bread, milk, vegetables, and other foodstuffs increased in price 47% between 2011 and 2012 and continue to rise.[36] The limited availability and higher cost of chicken prompted additional public protests last year as well.[37] In October 2012, Iran banned the export of 50 staple goods

---

[28] See GAO Report, p. 32.

[29] Hashemi Rafsanjani, *Mehr News Agency*, April 28, 2013.

[30] "Iran Failing to Pay Back Loans, World Bank Says," *Market Watch*, July 19, 2013 <http://www.marketwatch.com/story/iran-failing-to-pay-back-loans-world-bank-says-2013-07-19?reflink=MW_news_stmp>

[31] See "Despite Being Economically Unfree, Iran's Economy Shows Resilience"

[32] Thomas Erdrink and Rick Gladstone, "Iran's Next President Faults Ahmadinejad on Economy," *New York Times*, July 15, 2013. http://www.nytimes.com/2013/07/16/world/middleeast/irans-president-elect-describes-a-bleak-economy.html?ref=global-home

[33] See GAO Report, p. 34.

[34] Sees Erdrink and Gladstone, "Iran's Next President Faults Ahmadinejad on Economy"

[35] See "Iran Police Clash with Protestors Over Currency Crisis," *BBC News*, October 3, 2012 <http://www.bbc.co.uk/news/world-middle-east-19812482>

[36] See "Despite Being Economically Unfree, Iran's Economy Shows Resilience"

[37] See "Iran Feature: We Have Restricted the Wishes and Ideals of the Nation to Worrying about Chicken," *Enduring America World View*, August 2, 2012 < http://www.enduringamerica.com/home/2012/8/1/iran-feature-we-have-restricted-the-wishes-and-ideals-of-the.html>

to ensure an adequate domestic supply.[38] Iranian households now spend half of their monthly income on food items on average.[39] Roughly 40% of Iranian families live below the poverty line according to the IMF.

Further eroding Iranians' standards of living are increasing housing prices: as of late March 2013, housing prices in Tehran and other cities had doubled.[40] Medicines and certain medical supplies are also in short supply and are therefore much more expensive. Between January and August 2012, U.S. exports of pharmaceuticals to Iran dropped by almost half.[41] Iran's Health Minister was reportedly fired in December 2012 after publically complaining about this problem.[42] In February 2013, Iran's official unemployment rate stood 11.2%, although more reputable estimates suggest it is closer to double that.[43] Then-Expediency Council Member Hassan Rouhani went further and asserted that unemployment in the cities is even higher – in excess of 30 percent.[44]

At the same time, however, the country's economic stagnation is not as significant as one might expect given the extensive nature of the sanctions and the mismanagement of the economy by the Iranian government. Only two days after Iran announced those troubling 2013 inflation figures, the Tehran Stock Exchange reached a new all-time high.[45] Some sources claim that the Stock Exchange grew 47% in 2012 despite the sanctions[46] while others consider this growth extremely doubtful.[47] For fiscal year 2014, Iranian government statistics

---

[38] See "Iran Economy On Road to Recovery As Domestic Production Grows," *Al-Arabiya*, April 24, 2013 <http://english.alarabiya.net/en/business/economy/2013/04/24/Iran-s-economy-on-road-to-recovery-as-domestic-production-grows-.html>

[39] See Yassamin Issapour, "Inflation and Iran's Regime," *Wall Street Journal*, July 4, 2012 <http://online.wsj.com/article/SB10001424052702304211804577504400138905994.html>

[40] See "Despite Being Economically Unfree, Iran's Economy Shows Resilience"

[41] See "U.S. Exports to Iran Rise Nearly One-Third Despite Sanctions," *Reuters*, Oct. 15, 2012 <http://www.reuters.com/article/2012/10/15/us-iran-usa-exports-idUSBRE89E04L20121015>

[42] See "Despite Being Economically Unfree, Iran's Economy Shows Resilience"

[43] See "Despite Being Economically Unfree, Iran's Economy Shows Resilience"

[44] Tabnak website, May 15, 2013

[45] See "Despite Being Economically Unfree, Iran's Economy Shows Resilience"

[46] See "Iran Economy On Road to Recovery As Domestic Production Grows"

[47] See Paul Sullivan, "Iran's Wizard of Oz Economics," PBS Frontline, October 5, 2012 <http://www.pbs.org/wgbh/pages/frontline/tehranbureau/2012/10/analysis-irans-wizard-of-oz-economics.html> and "Iran's Stock Market (TEPIX) vs. Economy, What's Really Going on?" Distressed Volatility, September 30, 2012 <http://www.distressedvolatility.com/2012/09/irans-stock-market-tepix-vs-economy.html>

– the accuracy of which can not be verified – report inflation has been halved to 18%, with unemployment down by a modest 1% from 10.4% to 9.5%.

Looking into 2015, it is worth noting what Emanuele Ottolenghi and Saeed Ghasseminejad point out in their December 22, 2014 *Wall Street Journal* analysis: in his draft 2015 budget, Rouhani appears to be seeking to raise significantly the funding for the intelligence agencies, the IRGC (Revolutionary Guard Committee) and the basij – in other words, for the regime's instruments of enforcement, domestic control very much included.[48] "His largesse to the Guards is a sign of continuity with the repressive past," the authors note. "It also means that the Islamic Republic will continue its aggressive expansionary regional policy through the IRGC's Quds Forces."

This outlay will do nothing to reinforce the seeming recent improvement in Iran's economy, an economy about which the most accurate overall conclusion to be drawn is that it has been significantly weakened but is not on the verge of collapse.

Already during past years, the impact of certain sanctions was blunted, in part, by waivers granted by the U.S. Department of State to several of Iran's major oil purchasers that allowed them to continue to purchase diminishing quantities of Iranian crude as they sought out alternative supplies. In December 2012, China, India, Malaysia, South Korea, South Africa, Sri Lanka, Turkey, and Taiwan received waivers for 2013 because of their ongoing efforts to "significantly reduce the volume of their crude oil purchases from Iran."[49] China, for example, was actively replacing its purchase of Iranian crude – which fell from 550,000 bpd in 2011 to 450,000 bpd in 2012 – with Iraqi crude, and other countries followed suit.[50]

Iran further mitigated the impact of sanctions by identifying creative ways to circumvent them. One common technique was to forge documents to make Iranian crude oil appear to be of Iraqi origin, thereby making its sale on the

---

[48] See Emanuele Ottolenghi and Saeed Ghasseminejad, "Iran's Repressive Apparatus Gets A Raise," *Wall Street Journal*, December 22, 2014 <http://www.wsj.com/articles/emanuele-otto-lenghi-and-saeed-ghasseminejad-irans-repressive-apparatus-gets-a-raise-1419281552?tesla=y&mg=reno64-wsj>

[49] See U.S. Department of State, "Press Release: Regarding Significant Reductions of Iranian Crude Oil Purchases," Dec. 7 2012 <www.state.gov/secretary/rm/2012/12/201683.htm>

[50] See "Time to Move from Tactics to Strategy on Iran," *The Atlantic Council Iran Task Force*, April 2013, p. 8.

international market much easier.[51] Iranian oil is also moved onto foreign tankers in the open sea once the tankers' tracking beacons have been switched off, making its movement and ultimate sale very difficult to track.[52] Such oil is then sold at a discount in international markets.

There is also a large market of Iranian oil in Fujairah, UAE, where many European firms use Swiss subsidiaries to broker deals and pick up Iranian crude in tankers flagged under other jurisdictions.[53] Iran has also attempted to register its oil tankers in the Caribbean and Central America and hide their true country of origin, thereby bypassing the sanctions.[54]

Iranian companies also regularly ordered equipment and supplies that were otherwise blocked by the sanctions by listing Dubai as the final destination of shipment. They then hired local middlemen to transport the goods from the UAE to Iran.[55] To skirt the financial aspects of the sanctions, many Iranian importers used a network of Iranian go-betweens who own companies in foreign jurisdictions to make payments into the Western bank accounts of suppliers. The Iranian private sector, broader Diaspora, and even government entities regularly utilized *hawala* and other informal methods to transfer funds and complete this type of transaction.[56] These methods are both time-consuming and expensive and can reportedly require up to 30% of a company's revenue to pay all of the associated transaction costs.[57]

Sanctions also forced Iran to diversify its exports away from hydrocarbons and into electronics, automobiles, construction materials, etc., and it is reportedly gaining market share in other Middle Eastern and Asian countries as a

---

[51] See "Dodging Sanctions in Iran: Around the Block," *The Economist*, March 30, 2013 <http://www.economist.com/news/business/21574540-how-iranian-companies-manage-keep-trading-foreigners-around-block>

[52] See "Dodging Sanctions in Iran: Around the Block"

[53] See "Dodging Sanctions in Iran: Around the Block"

[54] See Benoit Faucon, "West Seeks to Plug Loopholes in Iran Shipping Sanctions," *Wall Street Journal*, October 15, 2012 <http://online.wsj.com/article/SB10000872396390443675404578057860497278752.html>

[55] See "Dodging Sanctions in Iran: Around the Block"

[56] See Najmeh Bozorgmehr and Lina Saigol, "Iran Finds Ways to Sidestep Sanctions," *Financial Times*, August 14, 2012 < http://www.ft.com/cms/s/0/60bcb7b6-e470-11e1-affe-00144feab49a.html#axzz2XWRffKl6>

[57] See "Dodging Sanctions in Iran: Around the Block"

result.[58] In late March 2013, the Iranian government announced that non-oil exports had already risen 20% in 2013 over the previous year.[59] And imports have reportedly decreased by 14% as domestic production has increased.[60]

Lastly, Iran continues to maintain its market-leading position in Islamic finance: in fact, roughly 50% of all global *Shari'ah*-compliant banking assets – valued at roughly $750 billion – will pass through Iran's financial system in 2013. This contributes to stable domestic liquidity of $346 billion and foreign exchange reserves estimated at $100 billion.[61] IMF forecasts predict that Iran's reserves will fall to $84.6 billion in 2013, however.[62] Iran also converts rials into hard currency in neighboring Afghanistan and Iraq, countries where large-scale U.S. deployments introduced an ample supply of dollars.[63]

Iran's economy has been noticeably impacted by international sanctions but will likely continue to muddle along, with its weakness a source of growing popular dismay.

The easing of sanctions will, at a minimum, buy the government time as the public is likely to show a degree of patience in waiting for improvements to become noticeable. At the same time, the government must make optimal use of this time period, as they will no longer be able to hide any incompetence and mismanagement behind the argument that sanctions are to blame.

1.4: Corruption

Corruption has been on the rise in Iran and is a contributing factor to its economic woes. Public dissatisfaction over corruption, especially with the IRGC's large-scale smuggling activities, has prompted periodic protests and labor strikes in Iran.[64] The clerical regime and IRGC have grown wealthy through their domination of certain sectors of the economy and control over tax-exempt foun-

---

[58] See "Despite Being Economically Unfree, Iran's Economy Shows Resilience"

[59] See "Iran Economy On Road to Recovery As Domestic Production Grows"

[60] See "Iran Economy On Road to Recovery As Domestic Production Grows"

[61] See "Despite Being Economically Unfree, Iran's Economy Shows Resilience"

[62] See GAO Report, p. 36.

[63] See Matthew Rosenberg and Annie Lowery, "Iranian Currency Traders Find Haven in Afghanistan," *New York Times*, August 17, 2012 < http://www.nytimes.com/2012/08/18/world/middleeast/iranian-currency-flows-into-afghanistan-markets.html?pagewanted=all>

[64] See "Despite Being Economically Unfree, Iran's Economy Shows Resilience"

dations.[65] The "murky" transfer of profitable state-owned assets to the IRGC was made possible through the government's abolition of independent financial watchdogs in 2012.[66] Some estimates assert that the IRGC controls roughly one half of Iran's entire economy, including most imports/exports, ports and terminals, manufacturing facilities, etc.[67]

Transparency International now ranks Iran 133 out of 176 countries worldwide (Iran is the 44th most corrupt country) in terms of perceptions of public corruption.[68] And The Heritage Foundation ranks Iran 168 out 177 countries worldwide in terms of economic freedom (or the lack thereof), which is due in large part to "rampant corruption" and government interference in its economy.[69] Corruption permeates all branches of government, including the judiciary, and bribery and cronyism are common obstacles to the fair adjudication of disputes in Iranian courts.[70]

Corruption has also tainted Iran's financial system. Iran suffered its largest banking scandal in its history in late 2011 when over $3 billion was embezzled from Iranian banks by a financier with close ties to then-President Ahmadinejad. Over 30 people have since been arrested, the head of one of Iran's largest state-owned bank has since fled Iran, and several senior officials at the Central Bank are under investigation.[71]

1.5: Iran's Domestic Policy

Iran's domestic policy is defined by its strict limitation of political freedoms and pervasive violation of civil liberties. Particularly harsh conditions are imposed upon regime critics and opponents, including journalists, civil society ac-

---

[65] See Freedom House, "Freedom in the World 2013: Iran," p. 2.

[66] See Freedom House Report, p. 2.

[67] Abbas Milani, "Taking Tehran's Temperature: One Year On," Carnegie Endowment for International Peace, June 8, 2010, http://carnegieendowment.org/files/0609carnegie-tehran.pdf

[68] See Transparency International, "Corruption by Country: Iran," <http://www.transparency.org /country#IRN_DataResearch_SurveysIndices>

[69] See The Heritage Foundation, "Iran," 2013 *Index of Economic Freedom*, The Heritage Foundation: Washington, DC, 2013, p. 249-250. [Economic Freedom Report]

[70] See Economic Freedom Report, p. 249-250.

[71] See Mike Shuster, "Iran's Largest Banks Swindled out of $2.6 Billion," *National Public Radio*, October 27, 2011 <http://www.npr.org/2011/10/27/141729872/irans-largest-banks-swindled-out-of-2-6-billion>

tivists, and human rights defenders, as well as women and minority groups.[72] A principal arm of regime control is its Ministry of Intelligence and Security. In addition to domestic monitoring and various repressive measures, its activities have included assassinations of dissidents outside Iran.

Since 2009, the government has increased its control over domestic Internet usage and deployed its security forces to crack down on public protests. Numerous journalists and leading opposition politicians, including unsuccessful presidential candidates from the 2009 election, remain imprisoned or under house arrest. The UN Special Rapporteur, who has been barred entry into to Iran since his position was created in 2011, documents Iran's ongoing human rights abuses, which have created a "culture of impunity" in the country.[73]

Iran's June 14, 2013 presidential election was the latest test of an electoral system that has proven itself to be "unfree, unfair, and unpredictable."[74] Historically, the state controlled elections by disqualifying candidates deemed disloyal or too liberal via its system of *velayat-e faqih*. The manipulation of elections outcomes typically happened in the Guardian Council before the elections were held. Indeed, in the June 2013 election, most candidates were disqualified by the regime at earlier stages of the process such that only a very small, regime-approved roster of candidates ultimately stood for election.

The government's security apparatus has long targeted reformist voices to consolidate its power.[75] Many Iran observers believe that the Iranian government engaged in voter fraud during the first round of the 2005 presidential election to force a runoff that allowed its preferred candidate (the then-little known mayor of Tehran, Mahmoud Ahmadinejad) to win.[76] The 2009 presidential election witnessed allegations of widespread fraud that ultimately tainted the election outcome and further undermined the legitimacy of Iran's political system. In the lead-up to the June 12, 2009 vote, Mir Hossein Mousavi, a former prime minis-

---

[72] See U.S. Department of State, "2012 Human Rights Reports: Iran," <http://www.state.gov/j/drl/rls/hrrpt/2012/nea/204359.htm > p. 1. [State Department Human Rights Report]

[73] See United Nations Human Rights Council, "Report of the Special Rapporteur on the situation of Human Rights in the Islamic Republic of Iran (A/HRC/22/56)," February 22, 2013, para. 3 [UN Human Rights Report]

[74] See Interview with Karim Sadjapour, "Iran's New Year Challenges," *Council on Foreign Relations*, March 27, 2013 <http://www.cfr.org/iran/irans-new-year-challenges/p30334>

[75] See Yasmin Alem and Barbara Slavin, "Iran's Internal Politics: The Supreme Leader Grows Ever Lonlier at the Top," Atlantic Council, p. 3

[76] See Alem and Slavin, "Iran's Internal Politics," p. 3.

ter from the 1980s, appeared to be the front-runner.[77] However, only hours after the polls closed, the incumbent was declared the winner with 63% of the vote. Large-scale demonstrations rocked Iran over the next eight months as millions of Iranians took to the streets to protest not only the vote-rigging but to question the fundamental legitimacy of the regime. The government responded with a violent crackdown and widespread arrests, including arrests of the candidates who alleged election fraud. Many political prisoners from the 2009 protests, including presidential candidates Mehdi Karoubi and Mir Hossein Mousavi, remain under house arrest four years later despite widespread criticism from the international community.[78]

Iran sought to avoid any unrest during the 2012 parliamentary elections by deploying a large number of security forces and engaging in widespread intimidation.[79] As a result, the tightly controlled election amounted to little more than "a contest between rival factions within the conservative leadership."[80]

Freedom of expression is extremely limited in Iran. All opposition groups are banned, and no print medium can publish an opposition viewpoint. Opposition websites are regularly shut down, and censorship even extends to publications belonging to peripheral factions within the regime. The Ministry of Culture must approve all books; roughly 250 "subversive" titles were banned in advance of the 2012 Tehran Book Fair.[81] For example, in 2012, Iran revoked the operating license of Chesmeh Publications, one of the country's largest publishing houses.[82]

The government also controls all television and radio outlets in the country. The authorities routinely issue orders that ban media coverage of specific events and/or topics, including the detention of opposition politicians, impact of the economic sanctions, and international criticism of the country's nuclear program.[83] Law prohibits participation in Persian-language satellite stations based outside of Iran, and at least one prominent economic analyst is serving a jail

---

[77] See Alem and Slavin, "Iran's Internal Politics," p. 4.
[78] See UN Human Rights Report, para. 13.
[79] See Alem and Slavin, "Iran's Internal Politics," p. 4.
[80] See "Freedom in the World 2013: Iran," p. 1.
[81] See "Freedom in the World 2013: Iran," p. 2.
[82] See "Freedom in the World 2013: Iran," p. 2.
[83] See State Department Human Rights Report, p. 24.

sentence for appearing on BBC Persia. [84]

Iran's 1986 Press Law lists 17 categories of prohibited content, which allow the regime to persecute independent journalists.[85] The Press Court has broad powers to detain and prosecute journalists for a range of vague offenses, including "insulting legal or real persons who are lawfully respected" and use of "suspicious sources."[86] Several newspapers and other publications were closed by the regime in 2012 on trumped-up morality or security grounds, including the independent newspaper *Maghreb* that was shuttered for publishing a cartoon depicting the president.[87] In September 2012, a court found Reuters Bureau Chief Parisa Hafezi guilty of "spreading lies" for a story she wrote about women practicing martial arts in Iran and suspended Reuters's accreditation in the country.[88] According to the Committee to Protect Journalists, Iran ranks second in the world in terms of number of journalists jailed (as of late 2012).[89]

In the run-up to the 2012 parliamentary elections, Iran increasingly targeted journalists and media figures. It arrested ten journalists and bloggers before the vote, five of which were accused of working for the BBC Persian Network.[90] One blogger was sentenced to a 14-year prison term for criticizing the government on his blog.[91] The government went so far as to harass, question, and detain family members of Iranian journalists based overseas.[92]

Iran also began to clamp down on the Internet following the 2009 elections by instituting new laws to persecute dissidents for online writings and strengthen the state's censorship of content.[93] Iran significantly increased its surveillance and control of Internet usage by blocking content and arresting Internet users for

---

[84] See "Freedom in the World 2013: Iran," p. 2.

[85] See UN Human Rights Reports, para 15.

[86] See "Freedom in the World 2013: Iran," p. 2.

[87] See "Freedom in the World 2013: Iran," p. 2.

[88] See "Freedom in the World 2013: Iran," p. 2.

[89] See Committee to Protect Journalists, "2012 Prison Census," December 1, 2012 <http://cpj.org/imprisoned/2012.php>

[90] See Rick Gladstone and Artin Afkhami, "Pattern of Intimidation Seen in Arrests of Iranian Journalists and Bloggers," *New York Times*, January 25, 2012 <http://www.nytimes.com/2012/01/26/world/middleeast/iran-steps-up-arrests-of-journalists-and-bloggers.html?pagewanted=all>.

[91] See UN Human Rights Report, para 16.

[92] See "Iran 'Detains Alleged BBC Persian Journalists'," *BBC News*, February 7, 2012 <http://www.bbc.co.uk/news/world-middle-east-16922285>

[93] See "Freedom in the World 2013: Iran," p. 3.

messages posted online.[94] The 2010 Computer Crimes Law criminalizes many forms of online expression and permits widespread government surveillance of the Internet.[95] During the 2012 parliamentary elections, authorities shut down access to various social networking, news, and email sites to prevent the opposition from using them to organize.[96] In January 2012, Iran rolled out a new regulation that requires Internet café owners to record the personal information and browsing history of customers.[97] Iran's most high profile initiative is the creation of a national *Halal* intranet that is disconnected from the global Internet and is completely controlled by the government.

Freedom of religion is extremely limited. The constitution recognizes several religious minorities, including Jews, Christians, and Zoroastrians; they are nominally allowed to practice their faith as long as they do not proselytize, but are discriminated against.[98] They are barred from most government and military positions, overtly disadvantaged in educational and work-place settings, and limited in the amount of property they can own.[99]

Conversion from Islam to a non-Muslim faith is punishable by death. Last year, the government shut down several churches in Iran's major population centers because they offered services in Persian, which according to the government, could have made them attractive to potential converts.[100]

Religious freedom is also limited for Iran's Muslims. A Special Clerical Court, discussed earlier in this chapter, regularly targets clerics who disagree with the Supreme Leader or otherwise advocate a different interpretation of Islam. For example, the prominent cleric Ayatollah Seyed Hossein Kazemeini Boroujerdi is currently serving an 11-year jail term for advocating the separation of religion and politics.[101]

Likewise, Sufi Muslims are persecuted for their beliefs. The leader of Iran's

---

[94] See State Department Human Rights Report, p. 1.
[95] See "Freedom in the World 2013: Iran," p. 3.
[96] See Alem and Slavin, "Iran's Internal Politics," p. 5.
[97] See "Freedom in the World 2013: Iran," p. 3.
[98] See "Freedom in the World 2013: Iran," p. 3.
[99] See U.S. Department of State, "2011 Report on International Religious Freedom: Iran Country Report," July 30, 2012 <http://www.state.gov/j/drl/rls/irf/2011/nea/192883.htm>
[100] See "Freedom in the World 2013: Iran," p. 3.
[101] See "Freedom in the World 2013: Iran," p. 3.

Sufis was arrested in 2009 and is currently serving a four-year jail term.[102] Iran's large Baha'i community – numbering some 350,000 persons – is the worst off of all of Iran's religious minorities and is systematically persecuted. They are not recognized under Iran's constitution, are denied almost all rights under law, and are actively prohibited from practicing their religion.[103] Under President Ahmadinejad, the security forces have intimidated, imprisoned, and attacked Baha'i communities on a regular basis.[104] Baha'i students are barred from attending university and denied access to their educational records. In January 2012, an appeals court sentenced six volunteer Baha'i teachers and instructors to four years in prison for participating in an online university project.[105] By the end of 2012, 110 Baha'is had been imprisoned, including several community leaders who are serving 20-year sentences for "espionage" and "engaging in propaganda against Islam."[106]

The Iranian government also targets and oppresses Iran's Ahwazi Arab minority. The Ahwazi complain of arbitrary arrest, detention, and prosecution for cultural activities.[107] The UN reports that the regime went so far as to arrest 130 Ahwazi attendees of the funeral for an Ahwazi poet, Sattar Sayahi, who died under suspicious circumstances after being detained by the Ministry of Intelligence in November 2012.[108] Several Ahwazi activists have received death sentences on charges of "enmity against God."[109]

Sunnis, who make up roughly ten percent of Iran's population, are in theory entitled to equal treatment under the law, but in reality suffer profound religious discrimination.[110] There is no Sunni mosque in Tehran, and Sunnis are gener-

---

[102] See "Freedom in the World 2013: Iran," p. 3.

[103] See UN Human Rights Report, para. 62-64.

[104] See "2011 Report on International Religious Freedom: Iran"

[105] See "Freedom in the World 2013: Iran," p. 3.

[106] See UN Human Rights Report, para. 61.

[107] See "2011 Report on International Religious Freedom: Iran"

[108] See UN Human Rights Report, para. 55.

[109] At the beginning of 2013, the UN Special Rapporteur on the situation of human rights in the Islamic Republic of Iran submitted an official protest against the planned execution of five Ahwazi activists. See Sung Un Kim, "UN rights experts urge Iran not to execute Ahwazi activists," *Jurist*, January 28, 2013 <http://jurist.org/paperchase/2013/01/un-rights-experts-urge-iran-not-to-execute-ahwazi-activists.php>

[110] "Iran's war on Sunni Muslims," *The Guardian*, October 16, 2008 <http://www.guardian.co.uk/commentisfree/2008/oct/16/iran-humanrights>

ally barred from senior government positions.[111] Iran specifically targets Balochi communities, which are Sunni, through "systematic social, racial, religious, and economic discrimination."[112] The government withholds funds to develop Sistan-Balochistan, thereby ensuring that Balochis have the highest poverty and infant mortality rates in Iran.[113] Destruction of Sunni mosques and religious schools and the targeting of Balochi clerics have been widely reported, too.[114] In May 2012, for example, the regime killed several Sunni Balochi protestors in Southeastern Iran who were protesting the arrest of a leading religious figure.[115]

Iran's female population is highly educated but is a constant target of government discrimination.[116] Women hold only 3% of parliamentary seats and are regularly blocked from seeking senior positions in government.[117] One of the few positions women are allowed to hold in government are judgeships; but women judges are not allowed to issue final decisions.[118] Women are not allowed to obtain a passport without the permission of a husband or male relative and do not receive equal treatment under Iran's *Shari'ah* laws on divorce, inheritance, and custody rights.[119] In addition, a woman's testimony in court is afforded only half the weight of a man's, and injury or death to a woman is only compensated half that of a man.[120]

Iran's judicial system cannot be termed either independent or fair. Arbitrary arrest and detention are commonplace. Suspected regime opponents are often held in unofficial detention centers for extended periods of time, and are subjected to torture and other physical abuse during interrogation. Numerous human rights reports document the pervasiveness of disappearances, cruel treatment, politically motivated violence, arbitrary arrest, torture, and a host of other of-

---

[111] See "2011 Report on International Religious Freedom: Iran"
[112] See UN Human Rights Report, para. 56.
[113] See UN Human Rights Report, para. 56.
[114] See "2011 Report on International Religious Freedom: Iran"
[115] See "Protests In Sunni-Majority Iranian Province Turn Deadly," *RFERL*, May 17, 2012 <http://www.rferl.org/content/protests-sunni-majority-iranian-province-deadly/24583918.html>
[116] See UN Human Rights Report, para. 40-44.
[117] See "Freedom in the World 2013: Iran," p. 3.
[118] See "Freedom in the World 2013: Iran," p. 4.
[119] See State Department Human Rights Report, p. 1-2.
[120] See "Freedom in the World 2013: Iran," p. 4.

fenses.[121] Relatives of regime critics are considered fair game, and spouses, siblings and children of dissidents are also regularly jailed, even if they personally did not engage in any activism. For example, several persons who were arrested during the 2009 anti-government protests were subsequently executed merely because of suspected affiliation with the *Mojahedin-e-Khalq* ("MEK").[122]

Of the 169 interviews conducted by the UN Special Rapporteur related to 81 cases of arbitrary detention, 76% of interview subjects alleged torture, both physical and/or psychological.[123] The most common forms of torture and physical abuse reported are rape, other sexual assaults, sharp force trauma, burns, electric shock, asphyxiation, and chemical torture; 60% of female detainees and 23% of male detainees interviewed reported rape.[124] It is not uncommon for arbitrarily detained suspects to die in custody, which is what happened to the blogger Sattar Behesthi in November 2012.[125] Prison conditions are very poor and have prompted hunger strikes by prisoners, such as in 2012.[126]

Trials commonly happen behind closed doors with the accused denied legal counsel. Politically sensitive cases are tried in Revolutionary Courts that routinely violate due process protections and issue summary decisions. It is commonplace for judges to accept coerced confessions and ignore torture or other abuse suffered during detention by security forces.[127]

Lawyers are pressured to abandon representation of regime opponents via harassment, intimidation, and incarceration.[128] Iran has systematically eroded the independence of the legal bar by – among other tactics – rescinding the law licenses of lawyers who represent political prisoners.[129] Human rights defenders are another popular target of government repression and are routinely arrested

---

[121] See State Department Human Rights Report, p. 1-2.
[122] See "Urgent Action: Two Men Executed, Amnesty International," January 26, 2011. <http://www.amnesty.org/en/library/asset/MDE13/010/2011/en/91fdfcc4-69d0-4e56-b9ff-575b639b82aa/mde130102011en.pdf>
[123] See UN Human Rights Report, para. 30.
[124] See UN Human Rights Report, para. 33.
[125] See UN Human Rights Report, para. 27.
[126] See "Freedom in the World 2013: Iran," p. 4.
[127] See "Freedom in the World 2013: Iran," p. 3.
[128] See State Department Human Rights Report, p. 1-2.
[129] See UN Human Rights Report, para. 21.

without warrants and physically abused.[130] Since 2009, 42 attorneys have been prosecuted for their defense work, including several prominent human rights attorneys.[131] In April 2012, one of the co-founders of the Centre of Human Rights Defense, founded by Nobel Prize winner Shirin Ebadi, was sentenced to a six-year prison term for, among other things, membership in a human rights organization.[132]

Among the hopeful expectations associated with the election of Rouhani was the notion that he would cause the regime in general to take a more liberal stance towards human rights and civil liberties. So far there is no sign of this. To the contrary, executions are reportedly taking place in even greater numbers than before. The vast majority of these death sentences are being handed down merely for activities seen as criticizing or opposing the regime. The prominent human rights activists Shirin Ebadi and Payam Akhavan have noted with disappointment that the nuclear negotiations have had no effect on "Iran's appalling human rights situation," but that executions, torture and religious persecution had instead increased under the new president.[133] Currently Western diplomats are acceding to Iran's demands that negotiations be restricted to a limited subject area and exclude – at least for the immediate future – both Iran's domestic human rights record and the broader problematic aspects of its foreign policy, including support to terrorist groups, incitement to the conflict in Syria, exacerbation of sectarian violence in Iraq and more. Several justifications are put forward for this exclusion: from the tactical argument that one should proceed gradually starting with the nuclear issue and then expand as confidence is built, to the pragmatist view that the internal situation of Iran is not among core Western interests. In Ebadi and Akhavan's view, an autocratic state with a strongly sectarian identity and a proclivity for aggressive foreign policy actions is not one that may be expected to respect nuclear deals. Nor, they argue, is it one whose violations of such deals could be tolerated in the expectation that it would handle its expanded capabilities responsibly.

---

[130] See UN Human Rights Report, para 19.
[131] See "Freedom in the World 2013: Iran," p. 3.
[132] See UN Human Rights Report, para. 20.
[133] See "In Iran, Human Rights Cannot be Sacrificed for a Nuclear Deal," *Washington Post*, November 30, 2013.

1.6: Iran's Foreign Policy

Iran's foreign policy transformed the country into a pariah of the international community, known principally for its evasion of international anti-proliferation efforts, its support of terrorist groups worldwide, and its domestic repression of cultural and political freedom. Viewed with a dispassionate eye and within the framework of its own goals and values, however, one must note that the regime has done well for itself, not only sustaining its power in the face of domestic unhappiness and great international pressure, but indeed building a position of regional supremacy through a combination of dogged determination and shrewd use of opportunities. Most recently it has used IS to its advantage, slipping deftly into the vacuum created by the Iraqi military's evident incapacity and the hesitancy of other countries – including the U.S. – to act. Today Iran has become arguably the preeminent foreign presence in Iraq, dominating its government and nearly running its defense. It is coming to be seen even by Sunni Arabs who otherwise would distrust this Shi'a state as more reliable in a crisis than the Sunni powerhouse Saudi Arabia or the global superpower United States. In the region, the Iranian regime is increasingly seen as one that sticks to its guns, is capable of determined action, and therefore must be accommodated.

Iran claims that its nuclear program is peaceful despite numerous reports by the International Atomic Energy Agency ("IAEA") to the contrary.[134] The IAEA has written at length about Iran's attempts to obtain technical information about the weaponization of highly enriched uranium, the structure of its nuclear weapons program, as well as how its nuclear facilities could be used to develop a nuclear weapon.[135] After repeated refusals to discuss IAEA concerns, Iran allowed an IAEA delegation to visit Iran twice – in January and February 2012 – but refused the delegation entry to at least once key nuclear weapons facility.[136] Since August 2012, Iran effectively ceased all cooperation with the IAEA.[137]

---

[134] See Institute for Science and International Security, "IAEA Report by the Director General: Implementation of the NPT Safeguards Agreement and Relevant Provisions of Security Council Resolutions in the Islamic Republic of Iran," November 23, 2010 <isis-online.org/uploads/isis-reports/documents/Iran_report-nov23.pdf> [IAEA NPT Report 2010]

[135] See Institute for Science and International Security, "IAEA Report by the Director General: Implementation of the NPT Safeguards Agreement and Relevant Provisions of Security Council Resolutions in the Islamic Republic of Iran," November 8, 2011 <isis-online.org/uploads/isis-reports/documents/IAEA_Iran_8Nov2011.pdf> [IAEA NPT Report 2011]

[136] See Katzman, "Iran Sanctions," p. 28.

[137] See Katzman, "Iran Sanctions," p. 28.

One key indicator of Iran's nuclear weapons program is its enrichment of uranium. As of August 30, 2012, Iran had enough low-enriched uranium to produce up to five nuclear weapons if it was further enriched to weapons-grade material.[138] Certain enrichment activities are pursued at the fortified Fodow site, which was only declared by Iran in 2009 after it was discovered by Western governments.[139] This location had originally been exposed by the Iranian opposition group the MEK in 2005, a report that was ignored at the time.[140] Iran's Bushehr reactor (discussed at greater length below) was fueled in 2010, connected to Iran's power grid in 2011, and was believed to be fully operational by 2012.[141] Iran is supposed to send the plant's spent nuclear material to Russia for re-processing, but there are fears that it could be diverted to Iran's nuclear weapons program.

Iran's nuclear program is a longstanding top priority of the regime that dates back to at least the 1990s, possibly earlier. In 1995, Tehran signed an $800 million contract with Russia to construct a nuclear reactor at Bushehr.[142] Little was known about Iran's progress until 2002 when information leaked by the MEK showed that it was building two facilities that could produce fissile material for a nuclear weapon – a heavy water plant at Arak and a uranium enrichment plant at Natanz.[143] The IAEA subsequently refused to provide technical assistance to the Arak facility out of a fear that it would contribute to nuclear proliferation.[144]

Diplomatic efforts to curb Iran's nuclear program following the revelations about Natanz and Arak similarly accelerated in 2002-2003. France, Britain, and Germany (the so-called "EU-3") secured Iran's agreement to fully disclose its nu-

---

[138] See David Albright et al., "ISIS Analysis of IAEA Iran Safeguards Report," *Institute for Science and International Security*, August 30, 2012 <http://isis-online.org/uploads/isis-reports/documents/Iran_report_--_August_30_2012.pdf>

[139] See Katzman, "Iran Sanctions," p. 30.

[140] See William Broad, "Iran Shielding Its Nuclear Efforts in Maze of Tunnels," *New York Times*, January 5, 2010 <http://www.nytimes.com/2010/01/06/world/middleeast/06sanctions.html?pagewanted=all>

[141] See Katzman, "Iran Sanctions," p. 30-31.

[142] See Katzman, "Iran Sanctions," p. 28.

[143] See Katzman, "Iran Sanctions," 28.

[144] See Katzman, "Iran Sanctions," 28. See also the interview of U.S. President George Bush, February 19, 2005, with *Le Figaro*. The French daily noted: "It was an Iranian group opposed to its government raised the alarm with the IAEA." Also see White House Briefing on March 10, 2003; White House Press Conference on March 16, 2005; *Los Angeles Times* on March 25, 2005.

41

clear program, sign and ratify the Additional Protocol to the Nuclear Non-Proliferation Treaty ("NPT") that allows for more invasive inspections by the IAEA, and cease all enrichment activities in exchange for peaceful nuclear technology.[145] Iran signed the Additional Protocol in late 2003 but never ratified it (and still has not at present) and stopped following its provisions after the IAEA reported in early 2004 that Iran had violated its NPT reporting commitments over the previous two decades.[146]

Iran signed the Paris Agreement with the EU-3 in February 2004 and again promised to cease its enrichment activities in exchange for continued talks against the backdrop of U.S. pressure for Security Council action and the recent U.S. invasion of neighboring Iraq.[147] That agreement broke down soon after Ahmadinejad was elected in 2005, and Iran rejected new offers from the EU-3.[148] On August 8, 2005, Iran broke IAEA seals on certain machinery and re-started uranium enrichment by early 2006.[149] The IAEA Board declared Iran in non-compliance with the NPT and referred it to the UN Security Council. Iran's non-compliance was acknowledged by the Security Council on March 29, 2006.[150]

In May of 2006, the Bush Administration agreed to join nuclear talks along with all other permanent members of the Security Council and Germany forming the so-called "P5+1." Iran was offered several incentives, including WTO accession and relaxation of certain U.S. sanctions on dual-use items, if it agreed to suspend uranium enrichment; it was threatened with sanctions if it did not. Iran was slow to respond and the Security Council passed Resolution 1696 on July 31, 2006, which required Iran to comply with IAEA demands.[151] Over the next two years, the Security Council passed four more resolutions – UNSC Res. 1737, UNSC Res. 1747, UNSC Res. 1803, and UNSC Res. 1835. Together, these resolutions banned the sale of weapons-related items, technology, and du-

---

[145] See Katzman, "Iran Sanctions," 31.

[146] See Katzman, "Iran Sanctions," 31.

[147] See International Atomic Energy Agency, "Iran-EU Agreement on Nuclear Programme," November 14, 2004 <http://www.iaea.org/newscenter/focus/iaeairan/eu_iran14112004.shtml>

[148] See Katzman, "Iran Sanctions," p. 31.

[149] See Katzman, "Iran Sanctions," p. 31.

[150] See United Nations Security Council, "Security Council, in Presidential Statement, Underlines Importance of Iran's Re-Establishing Full, Sustained Suspension of Iranian-Enrichment Activities (SC/8679)," March 29, 2006 <http://www.un.org/News/Press/docs/2006/sc8679.doc.htm>

[151] See Katzman, "Iran Sanctions," p. 33-34.

al-use to Iran; froze the assets of individuals and organizations linked to Iran's nuclear weapons program; and authorized the inspections of Iranian aircraft and ships suspected of transporting weapons-related items, among other sanctions.[152] Different incentives were also offered Iran for compliance with Security Council resolutions, to little avail.

The Obama Administration continued the P5+1 talks in 2009 despite the discovery of at least one new Iranian nuclear site that year. A new agreement was almost reached in October 2009 to allow the IAEA to inspect the new facility and France and Russia to reprocess much of Iran's low-enriched uranium for medical use.[153] Iran backtracked and ultimately did not sign. However, it did agree in May 2010 (against the backdrop of new sanctions discussions) to allow Turkey and Brazil to take much of Iran's enriched uranium in exchange for uranium reprocessed for medical use.[154] Still concerned by Iran's progress towards a nuclear weapon, the P5+1 soon thereafter introduced UNSC Res. 1929, which passed on June 9, 2010, and added new Iranian entities to the UN list; banned all travel for Iranian individuals on the list; created enhanced inspections of Iranian ships and aircraft; and banned the sale of most types of conventional arms to Iran, among other measures.[155]

Discussions progressed slowly in late 2010 and early 2011: little progress was achieved in meetings in Geneva and Istanbul. The issuance of a damning report by the IAEA in November 2011 (discussed above) prompted new sanctions by the U.S., Britain, and Canada that effectively shut Iran out of the international banking system.[156] In response, Iran's government backed mobs that ransacked the British Embassy in Tehran in late November. EU sanctions followed, effective January 23, 2012, that embargoed European purchases of Iranian oil.[157] The U.S. also implemented new sanctions, which expanded sanctions on financial institutions that engaged in transactions with Iran's Central Bank, thereby further isolating Iran's economy from global commerce. The impact of these sanctions is explored at length above.

---

[152] See Katzman, "Iran Sanctions," p. 33-34.
[153] See Katzman, "Iran Sanctions," p. 35.
[154] See Katzman, "Iran Sanctions," p. 33-34.
[155] See Katzman, "Iran Sanctions," p. 35-36.
[156] See Katzman, "Iran Sanctions," p. 37.
[157] See Katzman, "Iran Sanctions," p. 37.

In 2012, several rounds of talks were held. April talks in Istanbul yielded little concrete progress and follow-on talks in Baghdad in May were reportedly more substantive.[158] In Baghdad, the P5+1 reportedly offered Iran a supply of medical isotopes, much-needed aircraft parts banned by the sanctions, and international acceptance of small amounts of low-enriched uranium in exchange for Iran's halting all other enrichment activities, eventual closure of the Fodow facility, and a full inspection and verification regime.[159] Iran rejected this offer and follow-on talks in Moscow in June 2012 likewise failed to yield a breakthrough. See Appendix 1 for a chart that summarizes the key provisions of the various UN, US, and EU sanctions to date.[160]

The back and forth continues to the current moment, with March 2015 now portrayed as the prospective turning point, and perhaps it will be so. A reasonable, neutral observer is more likely to conclude that this is a game being deftly played by a patient adversary capable of taking a very long view. This adversary has already succeeded in entirely nullifying, not to say perpetually mocking, the very concept of a "deadline." Are we seeing a gradual erosion of Iranian determination to achieve weapons capability brought about by the persistence of international negotiators, or a seesawing towards precisely that capability on the part of Iran? The former is possible but the latter seems far more likely. At this writing, the U.S. Congress is once again pondering sharpened sanctions; some news reports are predicting a breakthrough with contested materials scheduled to go to Russia for processing. Iranian official statements are denying such an agreement, and yet another "deadline" has been rendered meaningless by yet another extension, as the drama goes into – depending on when one believes the program was launched – at least its 13th year. [161]

1.7: Iran's Role in Promoting Conflict in Iraq and Syria

Iran's most active foreign policy is in Iraq and Syria, where it mixes political

---

[158] See Katzman, "Iran Sanctions," p. 37.

[159] See Katzman, "Iran Sanctions," p. 37-38.

[160] See Katzman, "Iran Sanctions," p. 43-46.

[161] See the BBC overview, "Iran Nuclear Crisis: Can Talks Succeed" for a helpful, and sobering, summary. http://www.bbc.com/news/world-middle-east-11709428?print=true. For an assessment, see William Tobey, "The West is Getting Desperate in the Iran Nuclear Negotiations," Foreign Policy, September 28, 2014, http://foreignpolicy.com/2014/09/28/the-west-is-getting-desperate-in-the-iran-nuclear-negotiations/?wp_login_redirect=0

support with paramilitary assistance to empower extremists and prop up friendly Shi'ite-led governments. Tehran relies upon these two countries to project Iranian influence in the Middle East and to claim what it considers its rightful place as the leader of a Shi'ite axis. The survival of the Assad regime, in particular, is critical to Iran's foreign policy priorities. Tehran fears further isolation should that regime fall. Iran's intensive meddling in Iraq and Syria is a clear illustration of Iran's rejection of international norms and its persistent role in the destabilization of the region.

Iran and Syria have been strategic partners since the Islamic Revolution of Iran in 1979, and Syria is a lynchpin of the Resistance Front (*"Jabhat al-Muqawama"*) against Israeli and Western influence. Thus, Iran has a vested interest in prolonging the bloody civil war in Syria that has so far claimed over 100,000 lives.[162] Iran's active support of the Assad regime includes regular weapons shipments (through Iraqi airspace), large sums of money, and IRGC and other paramilitary advisors and fighters.[163]

Additionally, the war has reoriented the strategic calculus of many Iran-backed terrorist organizations, especially Hezbollah. Iran and Hezbollah are working together in Syria and have jointly spawned the pro-regime militia *Jaysh al-Sha'bi*.[164] Hezbollah has also increased its military involvement in the Syrian war and is now openly fighting alongside Syrian government forces to safeguard its and Iran's strategic reach in the Middle East.[165]

Iran is a major benefactor of Hezbollah, which was launched in 1982 under the patronage of the newly-established Islamic government of Iran and propped up by the IRGC. Hezbollah's presence in Lebanon provided Khomeini with more leverage in the Levant and a counterweight to Israeli and Western influences in the region. Hezbollah is, of course, a Lebanese organization actively

---

[162] See "Assad's Big Ally: How Deeply Entrenched Is Iran in Syria?" *Time*, February 26, 2013. <http://world.time.com/2013/02/26/assads-big-ally-how-deeply-entrenched-is-iran-in-syria/#ixzz2ZKtSACH9>

[163] See Molly Hunter, "Iraq Can't Stop Iran's Arms Shipments to Syria, FM Says," *ABC News* <http://abcnews.go.com/blogs/headlines/2013/07/iraq-cant-stop-irans-arms-shipments-to-syria-fm-says/>

[164] See "Assad's Big Ally: How Deeply Entrenched Is Iran in Syria?"

[165] See "Hezbollah Takes Risks by Fighting Rebels in Syria," *New York Times*, May 07, 2013 <http://www.nytimes.com/2013/05/08/world/middleeast/hezbollah-takes-risks-by-fighting-rebels-in-syria.html?pagewanted=all>

involved politically, militarily, and socially in the country, and it has maintained strong ties to Iran and has significantly affected Syrian and Israeli politics.

A U.S. Department of Defense report from 2010 estimates Iranian financial support to Hezbollah at approximately $100 million to $200 million annually.[166] Although Iran's financial capacity has decreased as a result of stricter economic sanctions, Hezbollah's financial needs have increased as it has sought to develop its weapons stockpiles and rebuild areas under its control following the 2006 war with Israel. In additional to Iranian funding, Hezbollah has constructed a complex global financial network spanning multiple continents.

Hezbollah is associated with multiple high-casualty terrorist attacks in the 1980s and 1990s, including the bombing of the U.S. embassy in Beirut in April 1983; the U.S. and French Marine barracks in Beirut in October 1983; the U.S. embassy annex in Beirut in September 1984; the hijacking of TWA flight 847 in 1985; and the attack on the Khobar Towers in Saudi Arabia in June 1996. Since 2011, Hezbollah has been tied to a number of foiled terrorist plots in Thailand, Bulgaria, Singapore, Kenya, Cyprus, and Azerbaijan as well as a failed attempt to assassinate the Saudi ambassador to the U.S.[167] Hezbollah has also been implicated in a bus bombing of Israeli tourists in July 2012, prompting the European Union to designate Hezbollah's military wing as a terrorist organization, which the EU had previously hesitated to do.

Iran's policy towards Iraq has undergone radical changes during the past decades. The two countries had very tense relations following the 1979 revolution and fought a protracted war with high losses from 1980 to 1988. Diplomatic relations between the countries were not restored until 2003 when the U.S. deposed Saddam Hussein's Sunni-led Baath government and oversaw the creation of Iraq's new Shi'ite-led government.

Dismantling the Iraqi Army and the administrative infrastructure of the country including its bureaucracy after the invasion of Iraq, coupled with allowing Iran's Iraqi proxies to enter Iraq, was an unexpected gift to Tehran. This allowed the balance of power in the region to tilt towards the Islamic Republic.

---

[166] See United States Department of Defense, "Unclassified Report on the Military Power of Iran," April 2010 <www.fas.org/man/eprint/dod_iran_2010.pdf>

[167] See Matthew Levitt, "Iran's Support for Terrorism in the Middle East," Washington Institute for Near East Policy, July 25, 2012 <http://www.washingtoninstitute.org/uploads/Documents/testimony/LevittTestimony20120725.pdf>

Since then, Iran's deep religious, economic, and social linkages to Iraq enabled it to significantly influence the other country's domestic politics. In this, it was able to capitalize on previously established relationships with many of the newly-empowered Iraqi politicians, including Nouri Al-Maliki (Iraq's prime minister from 2006 to 2014) and Jalal Talabani (Iraq's president from 2005 to July 2014), who had previously spent time in Iran as exiles or had otherwise required Iranian assistance in the past.[168] Since 2003, Iran has worked with Iraq's various Shi'ite parties, including more extreme elements of the Islamic Supreme Council of Iraq ("ISCI") and the Sadrists, and has cultivated relations with both major Kurdish parties to expand its influence in Iraq and steer Iraq more deeply into Iran's orbit.

These are normal diplomatic actions, and it is common for a country to seek influence over a neighbor. Less benignly, however, Iran also provided weaponry and training to pro-Iranian militias and terrorist groups that targeted U.S. forces and inflicted significant casualties with advanced IED technology and other support.[169] In particular, Iran's Qods force was active in Iraq and helped the Mehdi Army, Al-Sadr's militia, increase the lethality and frequency of attacks against U.S. targets.[170] Such attacks ceased after the U.S. withdrawal in December 2011, although Iran maintains residual paramilitary capabilities in Iraq. And Iran continues to use Iraqi territory to supply weapons to its allies in Syria.

At present, Iran still plays an active role in Iraqi politics but focuses its attention on targeting Iranian opposition groups in Iraq, most notably the MEK (discussed in Section 4.3 later in this report). Although the 3,400 MEK members residing at Camp Ashraf had been disarmed and were ostensibly under Iraqi government protection, the Iraqi security forces repeatedly attacked the camp after the U.S. handed control of the camp to the Government of Iraq in 2009; these incursions resulted in several dozen deaths.[171] Multiple mortar attacks by pro Iranian militias have also been launched against MEK members since the United Nations relocated them from Camp Ashaf to Camp Liberty in Baghdad

---

[168] See "Iran's Involvement in Iraq," *Council on Foreign Relations*, March 3, 2008 <http://www.cfr.org/iran/irans-involvement-iraq/p12521>

[169] See Kenneth Katzman, "Iran-Iraq Relations," Congressional Research Service, August 13, 2010. <http://www.fas.org/sgp/crs/mideast/RS22323.pdf>

[170] See Katzman, "Iran-Iraq Relations"

[171] See "Kerry Blames Iran for Attack on Iraq Camp," *AFP*, April 18, 2013 <http://www.rawstory.com/rs/2013/04/18/kerry-blames-iran-for-attack-on-iraq-camp/>

in 2012. Again, there have been casualties, and the attacks on unarmed refugees awaiting UN resettlement have drawn strong condemnation from the UN and from several European human rights organizations and national parliaments.[172] Hezbollah and Iran-affiliated groups have publically claimed responsibility for these attacks.[173]

1.8: Foreign Support of Terrorism

Iran has a long history of supporting foreign terrorist groups worldwide. The U.S. Department of State designated Iran as a state-sponsor of terrorism in 1984. In 2010, it also labeled Iran as the "most active state sponsor of terrorism".[174] Iran's financial, logistical, and material support of terrorist groups is funneled through the Qods Force, a branch of the IRGC, and spans the Middle East, South America, Central and South Asia, and Africa.

In addition to financial and logistical sponsorship of Lebanon-based Hezbollah (outlined in Section 1.7 above), Iran also provides material support and funding to Hamas, the Palestinian Islamic Jihad ("PIJ"), and the Popular Front for the Liberation of Palestine-General Command ("PFLP-GC") in Palestine. Hamas is a Sunni Islamist group that was established in 1987 and exercises control over the Gaza Strip, which was reinforced politically as a result of its success in the 2006 legislative elections. The group has maintained close financial and military ties to Iran, and in 2011 received Iranian technology to develop medium-range Fajr 5 missiles capable of hitting Tel Aviv. Similarly, in addition to the public funds associated with Hamas's political victory, Hamas has in the past received significant financial support from Iran to the tune of approximately $20 million to $30 million per month.[175] Hamas's withdrawal of its political headquarters in Damascus in February 2012 and its public condemnation of

---

[172] See "Secretary General Strongly Condemns Mortar Attack on Camp Liberty in Iraq; Calls on Government to Fully Investigate, Bring Perpetrators to Justice," February 9, 2012 <http://www.un.org/News/Press/docs/2013/sgsm14803.doc.htm>

[173] See "Shi'ite Iraq militia claims it attacked Iran group," *Associated Press*, June 17, 2013 <http://news.yahoo.com/Shi'ite-iraq-militia-claims-attacked-iran-group-123358565.html>

[174] See United States Department of State, "State Sponsors of Terrorism: Country Reports on Terrorism 2010" <http://www.state.gov/j/ct/rls/crt/2010/170260.htm>

[175] See Robert Tait, "Iran Cuts Hamas Funding Over Syria" *The Telegraph*, May 31, 2013 <http://www.telegraph.co.uk/news/worldnews/middleeast/palestinianauthority/10091629/Iran-cuts-Hamas-funding-over-Syria.html>

the Assad regime's crackdown on predominantly Sunni opposition groups has allegedly resulted in Iran temporarily discontinuing funding to Hamas.

Hamas's military wing, the Izz al-Din al-Qassam Brigades, has conducted numerous attacks against Israeli civilian and military targets since the 1990s using large-scale bombings, small arms, roadside explosives, and rockets aimed at Israeli territory.[176] The organization is believed to be responsible for the deaths of over 400 Israelis and at least 25 U.S. citizens since 1993.[177] PIJ media spokesperson Daoud Shihab has publicly acknowledged PIJ ties to Iran, stating in April 2013 that "[a]ll of the weapons in Gaza are provided by Iran, be they weapons intended for the Hamas movement or for the PIJ. Perhaps Hamas even has more Iranian weapons than us; and everyone knows that Iran is financing us."[178]

The PFLP-GC was created in 1967 following the Six Day War and was active in Israel and Europe throughout the 1970s and 1980s. The PFLP-GC has received training, logistical, and financial support from both Syria and Iran and maintains its headquarters in Damascus. There has been a recent resurgence of PFLP-GC activity that has corresponded with increased Israeli military operations in Damascus. The PFLP-GC announced in May 2013 that it would form brigades to liberate Israeli-occupied territories, specifically in the Golan Heights.[179]

Iran has also been active in the Tri-Border Area ("TBA") of Paraguay, Argentina, and Brazil with the support of Hezbollah and Hezbollah-affiliated entities there. There are approximately 25,000 Lebanese Muslims residing in the TBA, having emigrated from Lebanon after the 1948 Arab-Israeli War and the Lebanese Civil War that began in 1975.[180] A major hub for criminal activity and smuggling, the TBA has become an important source of Hezbollah's financing, and the lack of border control in the area facilitates movement of drugs, people,

---

[176] See National Counterterrorism Center, "Counterterrorism 2013 Calendar: Hamas," <http://www.nctc.gov/site/groups/hamas.html>

[177] See Jonathan Masters, "Hamas," *Council on Foreign Relations*, November 27, 2012 <http://www.cfr.org/israel/hamas/p8968>

[178] See Masters, "Hamas," November 27, 2012.

[179] See "PFLP-GC Says Forming Units to Fight for the Golan," *Ya Libnan*, May 12, 2013 <http://www.yalibnan.com/2013/05/12/pflp-gc-says-forming-units-to-fight-for-the-golan/#more-58155>

[180] See Pablo Gato and Robert Windrem, "Hezbollah builds a Western base," *NBC News*, May 9, 2007 <http://www.nbcnews.com/id/17874369/ns/world_news-americas/t/hezbollah-builds-western-base/#.UakJ9pyTvYM>

and funds. Hezbollah earns an estimated $10 million to $20 million annually from its activities in the TBA.[181] Hezbollah has also been implicated in a massive money-laundering scheme in South America that is apparently still active.

An Argentine prosecutor has launched an investigation into Iran's involvement in establishing terrorist networks throughout Latin America since the 1980s. Iran is also widely viewed as the mastermind of the bombings of the Israeli Embassy in Buenos Aires in 1992 that killed 29 civilians, as well as the bombing of the Asociación Mutual Israelita Argentina ("AMIA"), a Jewish community center, which resulted in the deaths of 85 people in 1994.

Iran-backed terrorist groups – Hezbollah in particular – have also established strongholds in Africa. West and Central Africa are home to a large, commercially active Lebanese Diaspora, estimated at over 100,000.[182] Large parts of this community are Shi'a, and some donate money to Hezbollah in the form of religious donations proffered to representatives traveling in the region. Hezbollah has used West Africa as a conduit for transfer of arms, funding, and drugs. Three Lebanese nationals allegedly connected to Hezbollah were arrested in Nigeria in May 2013 in connection with an armory of rifles, anti-tank weapons, and a rocket-propelled grenade[183] discovered in Kano, Nigeria, a commercial hub of Nigeria and one that has a large Lebanese business community.

In Afghanistan and Pakistan, Iranian IRGC train Taliban elements on tactical and logistical operations and weaponry, including small unit tactics, small arms, explosives, and indirect fire weapons, such as mortars, artillery, and rockets.[184] A relationship between the Taliban and Iran has developed since 2006 to include shipments of arms and ammunition from Iran to Taliban strongholds.[185] The relationship between Iran and al-Qaeda is more difficult to define, however.

---

[181] Gregory F. Treverton et al., "Film Piracy, Organized Crime, and Terrorism," RAND Corporation, 2009, xi <http://www.rand.org/pubs/monographs/2009/RAND_MG742.sum.pdf>

[182] See Hussein Dakroub, "Hezbollah Denies U.S. Claims it is Extorting Funds from West Africa's Diamond Trade." *San Diego Source*, June 30, 2004 <http://www.sddt.com/News/article.cfm?SourceCode=200406301ay>

[183] See "Nigeria: Hezbollah Armoury Discovered in Kano City," *BBC News*, May 30, 2013 <http://www.bbc.co.uk/news/world-africa-22722948>

[184] See U.S. Department of State, "Country Reports on Terrorism 2012," May 30, 2013 <http://www.state.gov/j/ct/rls/crt/2012/209985.htm>

[185] See U.S. Department of State, "Country Reports on Terrorism 2012," May 30, 2013 <http://www.state.gov/j/ct/rls/crt/2012/209985.htm>

According to the U.S. government, Iran has served as a safe haven for Iranian-based al-Qaeda networks and has enabled Muhsin al-Fadhli and Adel Radi Saqr al-Wahabi al-Harbi to operate a "core facilitation pipeline through Iran," creating a conduit for al-Qaeda to transport funds and militants through Iran to South Asia and Syria.[186] A report in the *Long War Journal* questions the relationship between Iran and al-Qaeda with regards to al-Qaeda's role in Syria, citing clashes between Iran-backed elements and al-Qaeda in the Syrian city of Qusayr near Homs, which prompted Mohammed Al Zawahiri, brother of Al-Qaeda leader Ayman Al Zawahiri, to commit attacks inside Shi'ite-led countries, including Iran.[187]

Iran has made recent efforts to engage in terrorist activities on the Indian subcontinent. Israel accused Iran of perpetrating a February 2012 attack against Israeli embassy personnel in New Delhi, India. The attack injured the wife of an Israeli defense envoy and three other passengers when a magnetic bomb under the vehicle was detonated. According to reports, India has resisted United States and European pressure to restrict trade with Iran due to its reliance on Iranian oil. As of September 2012, Indian officials have hit a dead-end in attempts to secure the arrests of Iranian suspects alleged to be connected to the attack as Iranian officials have not responded to repeated requests for assistance from Delhi police investigators to arrest three Iranian individuals.[188]

---

[186] See U.S. Department of State, "Country Reports on Terrorism 2012, May 30, 2013 <http://www.state.gov/j/ct/rls/crt/2012/209985.htm>

[187] See Thomas Joscelyn, "State Department Highlights Iran's 'Marked Resurgence' of State-Sponsored Terrorism," *The Long War Jounral*, May 31, 2013 <http://www.longwarjournal.org/archives/2013/05/state_department_ira_2.php>

[188] "India Hits Iran Dead-End in Israeli Terror Case," *The Hindu*, September 24, 2012 <http://www.thehindu.com/news/national/india-hits-iran-deadend-in-israeli-terror-case/article3932710.ece>

2. Trajectory of U.S. Policy

The Iran that exists today and the relatively robust sanctions currently in place are the culmination of various policies that have been pursued by the United States over the years. To properly understand the current context of Iranian politics and society and to appreciate the wide range of approaches that the United States has attempted vis-à-vis Iran over the years, it is worth reviewing the history of U.S.-Iranian relations since the Iranian Revolution.

The United States was caught by surprise by the Iranian Revolution in 1979, not having realized the fragility of the hold their ally the Shah had on his country or the rapidity with which he and the entire system of his government could be overturned. Experts also erred in their predictions about Khomeini, and had not anticipated his intention or ability to seize the reins of government and establish a clergy-dominated Islamic Republic. By the time most Western governments and experts understood what was happening, that new system was a fait accompli, and there seemed little alternative to accommodating the new realities.

This chapter will review the various attempts at coping with the new political realities in Iran since the Iranian Revolution in 1979. It will highlight how the U.S. tried every conceivable policy approach without bringing about any significant change in Iranian policy vis-à-vis the United States and U.S. interests.

2.1: Carter Administration

Immediately following the overthrow of the Shah's regime, the United States under President Carter made attempts to reconcile with Iran's new leadership and to put in place a viable working relationship between the two countries.[1] The efforts bore some initial fruit as a somewhat more moderate interim government led by Prime Minister Mehdi Bazargan and Foreign Minister Ebrahim Yazdi showed a degree of openness to America's attempts at establishing a dialogue.

But things took a more negative turn in October 1979. That month, President Carter, moved by a sense of obligation to a longtime U.S. ally, decided to permit the Shah to travel to the United States. The Shah was suffering from a severe case of lymphoma and had wanted and expected to enter the United

---

[1] See Gary Sick, "The Iran Primer: The Carter Administration," *United States Institute of Peace* <http://iranprimer.usip.org/resource/carter-administration-0>

States for medical treatment. The U.S. embassy in Tehran had advised President Carter not to allow the Shah to travel to the United States as the mood in Iran was generally hostile to the United States and such a move would only fuel the public anger.[2] And indeed, when the Carter Administration permitted the Shah to travel to the U.S, matters in Tehran spiraled out of control. Within a few weeks, a revolutionary student group stormed the U.S. embassy in Tehran and occupied the premises, taking hostage the U.S. diplomats who were in the compound at the time.

The hostage crisis and the resulting intensification of the conflict between Iran and the United States suited Ayatollah Khomeini. Khomeini and his fellow revolutionaries had been looking for the right time to press forward with their goal of instituting a new, theocratic constitution for Iran. But in the immediate aftermath of the revolution, there was no indication of substantial support within Iran for such a theocratic system of government.[3] That changed with the hostage crisis. As U.S.-Iranian relations deteriorated and Khomeini's rhetoric vis-à-vis the United States intensified, the Iranian public increasingly rallied around him as a figure of national pride who was standing up to the United States. Iran's moderate interim prime minister resigned, an indication of the overall radicalization of Iranian politics. And Ayatollah Khomeini consolidated control over the country.[4]

These developments limited U.S. options related to the hostage crisis. With Khomeini riding a wave of anti-American sentiment, he felt no motivation to take action in defense of the immunities that the U.S. diplomats in Tehran were supposed to enjoy.[5] Nevertheless, the Carter Administration launched a significant diplomatic initiative to have the hostages freed. President Carter sent letters directly to the Iranian government[6]; worked with allies in the region, who

---

[2] See Rose McDermott, *Risk-Taking in International Politics: Prospect Theory in American Foreign Policy*, Ann Arbor: University of Michigan Press, 1998, p. 84.

[3] See Massoud Parsi, "Iran's Anti-Secularist Backlash," *Al-Jazeera*, February 8, 2009 < http://www.aljazeera.com/focus/iranaftertherevolution/2009/02/200924101832660692.html>

[4] See "The Iran Primer: The Carter Administration"

[5] See United Nations, "Vienna Convention on Diplomatic Relations," 1961 <http://untreaty.un.org/ilc/texts/instruments/english/conventions/9_1_1961.pdf

[6] See "Document for November 6th: Letter from Jimmy Carter to Ayatollah Ruhollah Khomeini regarding the release of the Iranian hostages," *U.S. National Archives*, November 6, 2011 <http://www.archives.gov/historical-docs/todays-doc/?dod-date=1106>

pressured the Iranian leadership on the United States' behalf[7]; and leveraged the United Nations to deliver additional messages to the Iranian government. The United States even established a secret back-channel to the Iranian government through which it conducted direct negotiations.[8] And the administration exercised economic pressure by freezing various accounts at Western banks in an attempt to force Iran's hand. But none of these efforts succeeded in persuading Khomeini to release the hostages. Indeed, even negotiated settlements that were accepted by Iran's foreign minister were ultimately rejected by Khomeini.[9]

As a result, the Carter Administration began to look at various covert operation scenarios for rescuing the hostages. In the end, it settled on a plan that involved sending eight helicopters deep into Iranian territory. Various U.S. Special Forces teams were to link up with the helicopters once inside Iran. The Special Forces teams were to free the hostages and bring them back to the helicopters for extraction. Unfortunately, the mission ended in disaster. Several helicopters had to turn back before reaching the agreed-upon landing site due to various types of technical malfunctions.[10] A sandstorm made for limited visibility. Because of the mechanical problems and the sandstorm, the commander in charge of the operation was forced to abort the mission. As the remaining helicopters turned back towards their base, one of them collided with a transport aircraft and both crashed, resulting in the deaths of eight U.S. soldiers.

Due to the failed rescue attempt, the United States was forced to return to the negotiating table. At this point, the Carter Administration was approaching its final days. In part due to the hostage crisis, but in part also due to various other considerations, President Carter had lost his bid for reelection to Ronald Reagan, who had pledged, among other things, a more muscular foreign policy. The knowledge that Reagan would soon be taking over and that he would likely adopt a much tougher line towards Iran in the context of the hostage crisis served as an effective catalyst for the negotiations between the Carter Administration and the Iranian regime. Carter had a strong incentive to resolve the hostage crisis

[7] See "The Iran Primer: The Carter Administration;" and "Algiers Accords," January 19, 1981 <http://www.parstimes.com/history/algiers_accords.pdf>
[8] See Alan L. Miller, "Jordan Details White House Agony Over Iran Hostage Crisis," *Christian Science Monitor*, October 11, 1982 <http://www.csmonitor.com/1982/1008/100841.html>
[9] See "The Iran Primer: The Carter Administration"
[10] See "The Iran Primer: The Carter Administration"

before leaving office lest he end his presidency on an incredibly low note. The Iranian regime, meanwhile, did not necessarily want to give Reagan an excuse to start his presidency with a show of force against Iran to prove that his various campaign pledges about a tougher foreign policy were more than just rhetoric.

Consequently, in the very twilight of his presidency, Carter managed to secure a negotiated release of the hostages. The United States pledged to unfreeze certain assets, refrain from interfering in Iran's domestic affairs, and to refrain from taking any future legal action against Iran for its conduct in the context of the hostage crisis. In exchange, Iran pledged to release the hostages and to submit to a claims tribunal to adjudicate various commercial claims against Iran, in particular, claims by private companies resulting from assets that were nationalized during the Iranian Revolution. The agreement between Iran and the United States was finally signed on January 20, 1981 – the exact day of Ronald Reagan's inauguration.

It is important to note that the Iranian hostage crisis also had the effect of dividing the various Iranian political groups into two factions. One faction was strongly supportive of the hostage-taking, believing that the greatest threat to Iran's future was continued U.S. meddling in the country's internal affairs. This included the Tudeh Party as well as a majority of the Fedayeen (both groups will be discussed in more detail below), along with a variety of other groups with more Islamic tendencies. The second faction came to the view that the real threat for Iran was the return of another dictatorship under the pretext of struggle against the U.S. and the concomitant adoption of a more violent and reactionary turn by Khomeini. This faction included the MEK, the National Front, and the Freedom Movement of Iran, among others (these groups will also be described in more detail below). The groups of the first faction, in orchestration by the government, accused those in the latter of betraying the Revolution and conspiring with the United States. The hostage-taking incident provided Khomeini with a pretext for moving against critics under the guise of fighting the U.S. Bazargan's government was forced to resign.

Mousavi Ardabili, then-Chief Justice explained that "[The embassy takeover] brought about the fall of the Provisional Government, the isolation of the liberals and the confusion of left wing groups and the *Monafeqhin* (the regime term for the MEK). As Imam Khomeini said, this revolutionary move was greater than the first revolution."[11]

2.2: Reagan Administration

In addition to the freeing of the U.S. hostages that occurred on the day of President Reagan's inauguration, another significant development occurred around the same time that would affect U.S.-Iran relations. In September 1980, Iraq had invaded Iran, marking the beginning of the Iran-Iraq war – a war that would serve as the backdrop for U.S.-Iran relations throughout the 1980s.[12]

Prior to the Iranian Revolution, Iran had been one of the United States' key Middle Eastern allies in the Cold War, but that changed with the overthrow of the Shah. When Iraq invaded Iran, the United States initially had to consider whether to get involved and, if so, which side to support.[13] Initially, the Reagan Administration opted in favor of neutrality. Iran was no longer a friend, but Iraq was not an ally of the United States either. Saddam Hussein's Baathist party had socialist inclinations and had established at least weak ties to the Soviet Union. So it made sense for the United States to sit on the sidelines and wait to see how the conflict between the two countries would play out.

But by 1982, the tide of war was shifting decisively in favor of Iran. After repelling Iraq from Iranian territory, the Iranian government decided to push forward in an attempt to overthrow Saddam Hussein. From the U.S. standpoint, an Iraq and an Iran that balanced each other was a more stable solution than an Iran that was in charge of both. Such an Iran would effectively be a regional hegemon and would be able to run roughshod over other, smaller U.S. allies in the region, including Jordan, the various oil-producing countries in the Persian Gulf, and even Israel. So the United States decided to throw its weight behind Iraq. The U.S. government provided various forms of intelligence to Iraq and also worked with its allies around the world to prevent arms shipments from making their way to Iran.[14]

---

[11] Interview with Mousavi Ardabili on Tehran Radio, November 4, 1984.

[12] See Roger Hardy, "The Iran-Iraq War: 25 Years on," *BBC News*, September 22, 2005 <http://news.bbc.co.uk/2/hi/middle_east/4260420.stm>

[13] See Francis Boyle, "International Crisis and Neutrality: U.S. Foreign Policy Towards the Iran-Iraq War," Global Research, February 1986 <http://www.globalresearch.ca/us-foreign-policy-and-the-iran-iraq-war/5253>

[14] See Mike Shuster and Alex Chadwick, "U.S. Links to Saddam During Iran-Iraq War," *NPR*, September 22, 2005 <http://www.npr.org/templates/story/story.php?storyId=4859238>

Around the same time, the United States also suffered a massive terrorist attack that was orchestrated by an Iran-affiliated group. The terrorist attack occurred in the context of a U.S. peacekeeping mission in Beirut. Beirut had become embroiled in a regional conflict between Palestine and Israel. The Palestinian Liberation Organization (PLO) had been using Lebanon as a base of operations from which it was launching terrorist attacks on Israel. In response, Israel invaded Lebanon in attempt to break the back of the PLO. Iran ultimately sent roughly 1,000 Revolutionary Guard soldiers, which assisted in the creation of Hezbollah.[15] In the context of all this, the United States – as part of its support for a mediated end to the conflict in Lebanon – agreed to send a peacekeeping contingent to Beirut. That contingent was housed in a set of barracks, which Hezbollah attacked, resulting in the deaths of over 250 U.S. Marines.[16] In addition, Hezbollah took a number of Americans hostage, including several intelligence officers, in Lebanon in an attempt to intimidate the United States into withdrawing from the country altogether.

On the one hand, these incidents played a role in tilting U.S. support towards Iraq in the Iran-Iraq war. On the other hand, however, the hostages that were captured by Hezbollah gave Iran a degree of leverage over the United States, ultimately helping give rise to the Iran-Contra Affair. Motivated by a belief that there were certain moderate elements within the Iranian government with which the U.S. could deal more reasonably, the Reagan Administration initiated secret negotiations and ultimately authorized a covert program to send weapons to Iran via Israel in exchange for which these moderate elements would secure the release of hostages that were being held captive by Hezbollah.[17] The plan failed, the hostages were not released, and the entire affair became a scandal when it was uncovered in the United States. Indeed, it almost brought down the Reagan Administration.

Finally, in the late 1980s, Iran and Iraq began attacking each other's oil tankers in the Strait of Hormuz. Because this waterway is critical to the security of

---

[15] See Augustus Richard Norton, *Hezbollah: A Short History*. Princeton: Princeton University Press, 2007.

[16] See Jonathan Masters, "Hezbollah," *Council on Foreign Relations*, June 21, 2013 <http://www.cfr.org/lebanon/hezbollah-k-hizbollah-hizbullah/p9155>

[17] See "The Iran-Contra Affair," PBS <http://www.pbs.org/wgbh/americanexperience/features/general-article/reagan-iran/>

the global oil supply, the United States responded by beefing up its military assets in the region. The United States also went one step further, re-flagging Kuwaiti oil tankers as American and then escorting those re-flagged tankers through the Strait.[18] In October 1987, Iran struck one of these re-flagged tankers. In response, the United States sunk an Iranian warship and attacked Iranian oil platforms. Immediately after, in a tragic incident, the United States mistook an Iranian passenger aircraft for an Iranian military plane and shot it down, killing all 290 people on board.[19]

The Iranian people and government were incensed, but at the same time, they felt backed into a corner, exhausted by war. Running out of military supplies due to U.S. efforts to impose an embargo and increasingly feeling squeezed in the Strait of Hormuz, the U.S. bombing of Iran's oil platform in the Persian Gulf and the unfavorable status of the Iraq war, the Iranian regime decided after nearly three years to delay to accept UNSC Resolution 598 calling for a ceasefire agreement with Iraq in July 1988.

In the end, not much progress occurred in U.S.-Iranian relations during the Reagan years. If anything, relations deteriorated. The U.S. decision to back Iraq in the Iran-Iraq war helped turn the tide against Iran, a decision that to this day has not been forgotten by Iran. Meanwhile, the Hezbollah bombing of the marine barracks in Beirut as well as the various hostage-takings of American citizens throughout Lebanon were perceived by the United States to have been tacitly supported by Iran. Finally, the shooting down of an Iranian passenger plane by the U.S. military further inflamed an already volatile situation.

2.3: George H. W. Bush Administration

President George H.W. Bush took office amidst these rising tensions. In response, he sought very early on to take steps that would at least moderate the tone between the United States and Iran. Indeed, in his inaugural address President Bush again asked for Iran's help in reference to the hostages that were still being held by Hezbollah in Lebanon and said, "Good will begets good will; good

---

[18] See Bradley Russell et al., "Iran Won't Close the Strait of Hormuz," *Council on Foreign Relations*, January 4, 2012 <http://www.cfr.org/iran/iran-wont-close-strait-hormuz/p26960>

[19] See "U.S. Warship Downs Iranian Passenger Jet: July 3, 1988," *This Day in History* <http://www.history.com/this-day-in-history/us-warship-downs-iranian-passenger-jet>

faith can be a spiral that endlessly moves on."[20]

The initial focus of the Bush Administration in relation to Iran, then, was to secure the release of the U.S. hostages through an effort at cordiality. Unfortunately, progress on this front was slow at best. This was due to numerous factors. First, Ayatollah Khomeini died in 1989, the same year as President Bush's inauguration. This created a small political crisis in Iran and made it difficult for any Iranian officials to take meaningful actions on any major policy items, including the hostage issue.[21] At the same time, one of the more high-profile hostages that was being held in Lebanon at that time was killed in late 1989, further souring relations between the United States and Iran on the hostage issue. Finally, that same year, and shortly before his death, Ayatollah Khomeini issued his famous *fatwa* against Salman Rushdie for his novel, "The Satanic Verses."

All of these developments, occurring during President Bush's first year in office, put a damper on the Bush Administration's plans to alleviate tensions between Iran and the United States.

Over the next three years, matters recovered somewhat between the two countries. By 1991, all remaining U.S. hostages in Lebanon were released, which took that issue off the table once and for all. In addition, the U.S. invasion of Iraq served to accidentally align Iran's interests with those of the United States. Iran, after all, still despised Saddam Hussein for launching the Iran-Iraq war and generally favored any policies that weakened Iraq – the one country with the potential to challenge Iran for the status of regional hegemony.

But even these developments failed to restore anything resembling normalized relations between the United States and Iran. For one thing, Iran felt that the United States did not live up to its commitment to show goodwill in exchange for Iran's role in securing the release of the U.S. hostages in Lebanon. For another, Iran would have wanted the United States to go further in Iraq – specifically, they favored an overthrow of Saddam Hussein and support for the Shi'a uprising that occurred in Iraq's south following the U.S. invasion.

From the U.S. perspective, Iran was slow to assist with the hostages in Leb-

---

[20] See David Hoffman, "George Bush Sworn in as 41st President, Declares he will 'Use Power to Help People,'" *The Washington Post*, January 21, 1989 <http://www.washingtonpost.com/wp-srv/national/longterm/inaug/history/stories/bush89.htm>

[21] See Shireen Hunter, "Post-Khomeini Iran," *Foreign Affairs*, Winter 1989/1990 <http://www.foreignaffairs.com/articles/45135/shireen-t-hunter/post-khomeini-iran>

anon, which diminished the Bush Administration's appetite for demonstrating goodwill. Meanwhile, other developments, such as the Rushdie *fatwa* and continued Iranian support for quasi-terrorist groups throughout the Middle East, led the Bush Administration to conclude that the Iranian government was still not ready to be dealt with as a reasonable and serious interlocutor.

2.4: Clinton Administration

President Bill Clinton's first term was marked by numerous efforts at formulating a more muscular policy towards Iran. His administration identified Iran and Iraq as twin threats to U.S. interests in the Middle East, and it adopted a policy of containment towards both.[22] With respect to Iran, this meant a ratcheting up of sanctions, including sanctions that prohibited U.S. companies from engaging in any activities that would help develop Iran's oil and gas sector.[23] President Clinton simultaneously went one step further and issued an executive order that made it more difficult for U.S. companies to engage in any other trade relations with Iran. President Clinton's State Department, meanwhile, issued a travel warning in 1995 informing U.S. citizens that it would be dangerous for them to travel to Iran. And from a rhetorical standpoint, President Clinton also took a more forceful stance towards Iran, referring to the country as a "state sponsor of terrorism" and a "rogue state."[24] In fact, President Clinton was the first U.S. president to use the term "rogue state" in reference to Iran.

Matters between the U.S. and Iran almost came to a head in June 1996 with the Khobar Towers bombing in Saudi Arabia. In that tragic terrorist incident, a truck bomb was detonated within the Khobar Towers, a complex that housed a number of U.S. Air Force personnel in Riyadh. Americans determined within short order that Iran was involved in the attacks as intelligence reports indicated that the bombing was the work of a group called Hezbollah al Hijaz, a Saudi

---

[22] See Martin Indyk, "The Clinton Administration's Approach to the Middle East," *The Washington Institute for Near East Policy*, 1993 <http://www.washingtoninstitute.org/policy-analysis/view/the-clinton-administrations-approach-to-the-middle-east>

[23] See U.S. Department of the Treasury Office of Foreign Assets Control, "An Overview of O.F.A.C. Regulations Involving Sanctions Against Iran," <http://www.washingtoninstitute.org/policy-analysis/view/the-clinton-administrations-approach-to-the-middle-east>

[24] See Robert Litwak, *Rogue States and U.S. Foreign Policy: Containment After the Cold War*, Washington, DC: Woodrow Wilson Center Press, 2000, p. 4.

Shi'a group that had links to the Iranian Revolutionary Guard.[25]

According to Louis Freeh, former Director of the FBI who was in charge of the investigation, "It became clear that although the attack was operationally performed by the Hezbollah in Saudi Arabia, the attack was organized, planned, funded, and executed by the IRGC. They had gotten the passports for the operators. They had funded them with cash. The general in the IRGC, who was in charge of the project, sat in…the Iranian Embassy in Damascus, and gave them their passports."[26]

President Clinton considered various military options to respond to the attacks. Ultimately, however, he determined that the risks of conducting a military response to the Khobar Towers bombings were too substantial. According to one of President Clinton's principal advisors at the time, the administration "quickly recognized any operations could escalate and even trigger full-scale war."[27] As a result, the administration took somewhat more moderate measures. It warned Iran against taking any other provocative actions and moved additional military assets to the Persian Gulf. It also undertook a campaign to identify and disrupt Iranian intelligence personnel in various locations around the world.

Then, in 1997 during President Clinton's second term, Mohammad Khatami was elected president. Khatami's election came as a surprise: most observers were predicting that a more hard-line candidate would win. Khatami immediately struck a more moderate tone. In a CNN interview, he stated that Iran and the United States should create a "crack in the wall of mistrust" that existed between the two countries.[28] He professed his belief that "all doors should now be open for such dialogue and understanding and the possibility for contact between Iranian and American citizens."[29]

---

[25] See Carol Leonnig, "Iran Held Liable in Khobar Attack," *The Washington Post*, December 23, 2006 <http://www.washingtonpost.com/wp-dyn/content/article/2006/12/22/AR2006122200455.html>

[26] "The Foiled Plot to Assassinate the Saudi Ambassador In Washington: Exposing Iran's Islamic Revolutionary Guards Corps-Qods Force," *PRNewsWire*, October 17, 2011 <http://www.prnews-wire.com/news-releases/the-foiled-plot-to-assassinate-the-saudi-ambassador-in-washington-expos-ing-irans-islamic-revolutionary-guards-corps-qods-force-132006518.html>

[27] See Bruce Riedel, "The Iran Primer: The Clinton Administration," United States Institute of Peace <http://iranprimer.usip.org/resource/clinton-administration>

[28] See "Khatami: Crack Wall of Mistrust," *New Straits Times*, January 9, 1998, F-15.

[29] See "Khatami Suggests Warmer Relations with U.S.," *CNN*, January 7, 1998 <http://www.cnn.com/WORLD/9801/07/iran/>

President Clinton and his Iran advisers sought to explore whether this rhetoric presented a real opportunity to change the relationship between Iran and the United States. As a result, the Clinton Administration substantially moderated its tone towards Iran during its second term. President Clinton taped messages for the Iranian people for the Iranian New Year in 1997, 1998, and 1999 carrying messages of peace and reconciliation. In these messages, he offered his regret for the "estrangement of our two nations" and his hope that "the day will soon come when we can enjoy once again good relations with Iran."[30] In addition, as a conciliatory gesture, President Clinton in 2000 personally attended the session during which President Khatami addressed the United Nations General Assembly in New York. Later that year, Secretary Madeline Albright formally apologized to Iran[31] for the role played by the United States in the 1953 coup that overthrew Mohammad Mosaddegh and re-installed the Iranian monarchy. This may have pleased the Iranian public, among whom Mosaddegh was still widely viewed as a patriot; what the Iranian regime thought of this gesture, however, is another question, since they had been strongly opposed to Mosaddegh and his vision for the country.

The Clinton Administration also took a number of concrete actions to ease tensions between the two countries. The travel warning that had been issued by the State Department during the administration's first term was lifted, making it easier for U.S. citizens to travel to Iran. Certain sanctions – notably on Iranian exports like carpets, nuts, dried fruits, and caviar – were lifted. And the administration fostered various cultural and athletic exchanges between Iran and the United States. Most famous among these was the visit to Tehran by an American wrestling team. The members of the U.S. team were later invited to the White House for a photo opportunity with the president.

President Clinton also made several overtures to Iran requesting an opportunity to engage in direct talks. One such overture was an offer to the Iranian government – passed along through the Swiss Embassy in Tehran – to meet with three senior U.S. State Department officials without preconditions and at

---

[30] See "Clinton Send Conciliatory Message to Iran," *New York Times*, January 30, 1998 <http://www.nytimes.com/1998/01/30/world/clinton-sends-conciliatory-message-to-iran.html>

[31] See "Secretary of State Madeleine K. Albright Remarks Before the American-Iranian Council," Federation of American Scientists, March 17, 2000 <http://www.fas.org/news/iran/2000/000317.htm>

a time and place of Iran's choosing.[32] Vice President Al Gore, meanwhile, asked the Saudi government to arrange a high-level meeting between the United States and Iran. And at a multilateral conference hosted by the United Nations, Madeleine Albright sought to have a meeting on the sidelines of the conference with her Iranian counterpart. He never showed up for the meeting, however.

With respect to the Iranian opposition, a significant step taken by Clinton Administration in the first year of his second term was the designation of the MEK as a foreign terrorist organization ("FTO"). A senior administration official at the time acknowledged that the designation was a "goodwill gesture" toward the newly elected "moderate" president.[33]

In sum, the Clinton Administration's tenure was marked by a ratcheting up of pressure during the first term through various mechanisms – sanctions, rhetoric, and deploying military assets to the Persian Gulf – followed by a charm offensive and conciliatory gestures in the second term. Neither approach yielded tangible results in terms of inducing better behavior on the part of the Iranian regime.

2.5: George W. Bush Administration

The Bush Administration took note of President Clinton's efforts during his second term to reach out to the Iranian regime. However, it also took note of the Iranian government's lack of meaningful reciprocation. As a result, the Bush Administration was highly skeptical that such outreach could prove effective, and operated under the assumption that the Iranian regime was either unwilling or – perhaps due to various internal struggles within Iran – unable to reciprocate. Indeed, the lack of a positive response by Khatami was taken by the Bush Administration as evidence that he was unable or unwilling to deliver.

Despite this baseline skepticism, the Bush Administration engaged in substantial cooperation with Iran following the terrorist attacks on September 11, 2001. With respect to the Bush Administration's efforts to topple the Taliban, U.S. and Iranian interests converged and, as a result, U.S. diplomats and Iranian

---

[32] See "The Iran Primer: The Clinton Administration"

[33] See Norman Kempster, "U.S. Designates 30 Groups as Terrorists," *Los Angeles Times*, October 9, 1997.

diplomats worked closely together in crafting a common policy.[34]

Iran had long opposed the Taliban because of its political ideology and affiliations with Pakistan and al-Qaeda. As a result, the Iranian government had been backing the Northern Alliance for numerous years – the same group the United States threw its weight behind the campaign to unseat the Taliban in Afghanistan. At a conference in Bonn in 2002[35] after the Taliban had been ousted, U.S. and Iranian diplomats worked together to convince the Northern Alliance to support Hamid Karzai as an interim president of Afghanistan.

But alongside this alliance of necessity between Iran and the United States on the issue of Afghanistan, the Bush Administration ratcheted up its rhetoric towards Iran. Increasingly concerned about Iran's activities in sponsoring terrorist groups like Hezbollah and Hamas, President Bush, in his January 2002 State of the Union address, placed Iran in a group with North Korea and Iraq that he labeled the "axis of evil".[36] These were three countries that President Bush said were state sponsors of terrorism and that were pursuing nuclear weapons, a dangerous combination that he deemed unacceptable. And in the case of Iran, the country was already turning to training and arming Shi'ite militants in Iraq and subsequently Taliban insurgents in Afghanistan.[37]

And to be sure, around this same time, various sites in Iran were discovered at which the Iranian government was clandestinely developing a nuclear capability. The most shocking revelation came from the MEK in August 2002 when they disclosed the secret nuclear site at Natanz as well as the heavy water project at Arak to the United States. The IAEA then initiated a campaign to obtain access to these sites, in particular the uranium enrichment site at Natanz. Meanwhile, Great Britain, France, and Germany initiated diplomatic outreach to Iran in an attempt to broker a deal to achieve suspension of Iran's nuclear enrichment activities.

An agreement was signed in 2004 in which the Iranian government agreed to suspend its enrichment activities and give the IAEA greater access to its var-

---

[34] See Stephen J. Hadley, "The Iran Primer: The George W. Bush Administration," United States Institute of Peace, <http://iranprimer.usip.org/resource/george-w-bush-administration>

[35] See "The Iran Primer: The George W. Bush Administration"

[36] See "Text of Bush's 2002 State of the Union Address," *The Washington Post*, January 29, 2002 <http://www.washingtonpost.com/wp-srv/onpolitics/transcripts/sou012902.htm>

[37] See "The Iran Primer: The George W. Bush Administration"

ious facilities. In response to the signing of this agreement, the United States announced that it would no longer object to Iran's accession to the World Trade Organization and also indicated that it would consider providing various spare parts to Iran to update its fleet of civilian aircraft.

But shortly thereafter, two developments changed the situation. First, Mahmoud Ahmadinejad, supported by Ayatollah Khamenei, became Iran's new president. At the same time, the situation in Iraq had begun to deteriorate, confronting the U.S. with serious challenges. The latter was the decisive factor inclining Iran to take a more aggressive approach. With the U.S. preoccupied in Iraq, its threat to expand the War on Terror to include Iran had become less credible. Ahmadinejad, reflecting Khamenei's own position, disavowed the diplomats who had negotiated the 2004 agreement, and renounced the agreement itself. He announced that the country would again begin enriching uranium and, in 2006, Iran publicly made it known that enrichment activities had started up again at the Natanz facility.

The United States took several actions in response to this increased belligerence on the part of Iran. First, it sought to increase economic pressure on the country. In a series of resolutions that were passed by the UN Security Council, the United States spearheaded the installation of a sanctions regime that included sanctions on financial institutions, persons associated with the country's nuclear activities, and arms sales to Iran, as well as travel bans and other similar policies. The administration also launched a campaign to convince financial institutions around the world to pledge not to do transactions with Iran, which also made it difficult for multinational companies that bank with these financial institutions to do business in Iran.[38]

Second, it continued to back the diplomatic initiatives that were being undertaken by its European allies. In August 2005, for example, the same group of countries that negotiated the 2004 agreement sought again to extract a new commitment from Iran to give up its enrichment activities in exchange for substantial assistance from the European Union with respect to the country's civilian nuclear ambitions. And beginning in 2006, the P5+1 launched its own series

---

[38] For information on international support of Bush's sanctions, see Steven Myers and Alan Cowell, "European Leaders Support Bush's Sanctions," *New York Times*, June 10, 2008 <http://www.nytimes.com/2008/06/10/world/americas/10iht-11prexy.13608048.html?_r=0>

of negotiations.

Third, the Bush Administration sought to promote greater freedom within Iran with the hope that doing so could accelerate the demise of the Iranian government. Indeed, the George W. Bush Administration was the first U.S. Administration since the 1979 revolution to pursue regime change, at least at the rhetorical level and through a modest democracy promotion program. In his 2006 State of the Union address, President Bush referred to Iran as "a nation now held hostage by a small clerical elite that is isolating and repressing its people" and called on the Iranian people to choose their own future and win their freedom—a call that was interpreted as a call for regime change, although the administration did not use that language in public.[39] The Bush Administration was also the first to overtly open channels of communication to the external Iranian opposition. In July 2006, Elliot Abrams and Nicholas Burns met with some 30 democracy activists and members of Iranian opposition groups to discuss the future of Iran. The former Shah's son and a leading activist, Akbar Ganji, who was touring the United States, did not attend.[40]

President Bush also continued with the tradition established by President Clinton of sending messages of congratulations to Iran for the Iranian New Year, but he was always careful to distinguish between the Iranian people and the Iranian government – making clear that his good wishes were intended only for the populace, whose desire for greater freedom he supported. In public pronouncements, he condemned crackdowns on the Iranian opposition as well as other human rights violations that were occurring in Iran. In 2008, the administration worked with Congress to craft a bill that appropriated $60 million for efforts at supporting democracy in Iran. This followed earlier efforts by the Bush Administration to increase the free flow of information into Iran, including the establishment of the radio station Radio Farda and the beefing up of Voice of America programming for the country. The Bush Administration did not, however, engage in any meaningful efforts to back particular opposition groups or initiatives for fear of tainting the credibility of these groups. As former National Security Advisor Steve Hadley later explained, "The Bush Administration want-

---

[39] See Guy Dinmore, "Bush 'calling for Iran regime change,'" *Financial Times*, February 1, 2006 <http://www.ft.com/cms/s/0/d3a86bf0-9358-11da-a978-0000779e2340.html#axzz2V2d83M8M>
[40] See Eli Lake, "Iranian Opposition Divisions Mar Visit to White House," *The Sun*, July 21, 2006, <http://www.nysun.com/foreign/iranian-opposition-divisions-mar-visit-to-white/36528/>

ed to show that it stood with the Iranian people, but without discrediting Iranian political activists or subjecting them to the charge of being American agents."[41]

Fourth, it worked with allies in the region to beef up security cooperation in an attempt to deter Iran from moving forward with its nuclear ambitions. It also positioned additional military assets in the area, including, of course, assets along Iran's borders in both Iraq and Afghanistan. And the administration made sure to clarify that it considered a nuclear Iran unacceptable, stating further that it would keep all options on the table for preventing such an outcome.

As President Bush liked to say, in Iran there are two clocks: one that tracks Iran's progress towards a nuclear weapon, and the other that measures how much longer the Iranian regime can survive; with the goal of U.S. policy therefore being to slow the former while accelerating the latter. Accordingly, the Bush Administration's blend of policies towards Iran was designed to advance these twin goals. Unfortunately, there was not much success on either front. By the end of the Bush Administration, Iran had made unmonitored progress towards a nuclear weapon, and its government appeared no closer to collapse.

2.6: Obama Administration

Under the Obama Administration, U.S. policy has been one of outreach followed by a blend of sanctions and diplomacy. The outreach occurred during the first year of the Obama Administration in 2009. The most significant indicators were the New Year's greeting sent by President Barack Obama to the people and the leadership of Iran that year, in which President Obama pledged that he sought a "new beginning" in U.S.-Iranian relations[42] and that he was committed to resolving any outstanding issues between the two countries peacefully and through diplomacy; and, later that same year, the restraint shown by President Obama in response to the brutal crackdown by the Iranian government against the uprising. This approach inspired crowds to chant the slogan "Obama! Are you with us or with them?" in the streets of Tehran.

During his presidential campaign, President Obama stated that, in contrast to President Bush, he would negotiate with Iran's leaders without preconditions

---

[41] See "The Iran Primer: The George W. Bush Administration"

[42] See Ian Black, "Barack Obama Offers 'New Beginning' with Video Message," *The Guardian*, March 20, 2009 <http://www.guardian.co.uk/world/2009/mar/20/barack-obama-video-iran>

because he believed in dialogue, even with enemies. Then shortly after being elected, President Obama began to implement the more conciliatory policy towards Iran he'd promised. President Obama's New Year's greeting went substantially further than those of the Bush Administration. Rather than distinguishing between the Iranian people and the government and clarifying that the well-wishes were intended for the people only, President Obama addressed portions of his remarks directly to the Iranian government, stating that he wished to "speak directly to the people *and leaders* of the Islamic Republic of Iran" (added emphasis). He went on to say:

> In this season of new beginnings I would like to speak clearly to Iran's leaders. We have serious differences that have grown over time. My administration is now committed to diplomacy that addresses the full range of issues before us, and to pursuing constructive ties among the United States, Iran, and the international community. This process will not be advanced by threats. We seek instead engagement that is honest and grounded in mutual respect.[43]

Later that same year, President Obama gave his famous June 2009 address in which he stated that it was time for a "new beginning" between the United States and the Muslim world. With respect to Iran specifically, President Obama acknowledged "decades of mistrust" but said that he was ready to move forward with diplomatic engagement "without preconditions on the basis of mutual respect."[44]

Just one week after President Obama's remarks in June, however, the presidential elections took place in Iran. What followed were protests by Iranians charging that the regime had rigged the election. These protests set off a six-month spiral of ever larger demonstrations, followed by a matching escalation of regime crackdowns. Initially, the Green Movement – as this wave of protest came

---

[43] See The White House Office of the Press Secretary, "Videotaped Remarks in Celebration of Nowruz," March 20, 2009 <http://www.whitehouse.gov/the-press-office/videotaped-remarks-president-celebration-nowruz>

[44] See "Text: Obama's Speech in Cairo," *New York Times*, June 4, 2009 <http://www.nytimes.com/2009/06/04/us/politics/04obama.text.html?pagewanted=all>

to be known – blamed President Ahmadinejad for the stolen election and demanded that the regime either correct the election results or allow new elections. However, the people's demands went far beyond the positions supported by the Green Movement's leadership. As the demonstrations went on, the message became much broader and the demonstrators' anger was increasingly directed at the entirety of the regime, including Ayatollah Khamenei. Within a few weeks the slogan "Where is my vote?" had been replaced by "Down with Khamenei," "Down with the dictator," and "Down with *velayat-e faqih*." The showdown between the protestors and the highest echelons of the Iranian regime reached such a crescendo that many outside observers thought the regime was in its final throes. However, the regime fought back brutally and spearheaded an unprecedented crackdown on the protestors that ultimately broke the spirit of the people's movement. After roughly six months, the protests died down. Sadly, U.S. policy played a part in sapping the energies of the protest movement. Indeed, at a time when the Iranian people most needed international support, President Obama was extending his hand to the leaders of the regime – pointlessly, as it turned out.

Throughout this entire period, President Obama was slow to speak out on behalf of the protestors and against the brutal crackdowns that were occurring in the country. There is no doubt that President Obama was initially caught off guard and – before it was clear how significant the protests would become, and how brutal the crackdown – he understandably did not want to jeopardize his strategy of dialogue. As a result, the President initially refrained from issuing any comments on the protests or on the legitimacy of the election results.

As the crackdowns became more severe and the protests more determined, the President refrained from speaking out because he and his advisors wrongly thought that throwing the administration's weight behind the protestors might undermine their legitimacy as the Iranian regime would then be able to argue that the protestors were acting at the behest of the U.S. government. It was not until several months into the protests that President Obama finally spoke out against the massive and egregious human rights violations.

Since then, President Obama has held to his hope of solving the nuclear crisis through diplomacy, but he has been somewhat more willing to criticize and has become less sanguine about the prospects of outreach to the Iranian regime. He has authorized ongoing talks with the government while at the same time spearheading a campaign to impose even stronger sanctions on the country. Furthermore, he has repeatedly declared that a nuclear Iran would be unacceptable, implying that he might be prepared to authorize limited strikes to buy time. The goal of this overall policy is to use sanctions and the veiled threat of limited strikes as sticks that indicate to Iran that it has no choice but to reach a reasonable, negotiated settlement with the United States.

While some have offered credible arguments that the Administration – if it believes negotiation is failing – may ultimately dilute its position and choose containment of a nuclear Iran over targeted strikes, there is no sign that the Administration is aware of, let alone considering, a broader range of options such as destabilizing the regime to make it more amenable to compromise or of bolstering the opposition.

Private conversations with members of the U.S. government who are involved in setting U.S. policy towards Iran reveal deep skepticism towards the opposition in general. The opposition inside Iran is described by these U.S. government officials as "depressed and downtrodden," and as effectively being controlled by the regime. The Green Movement is considered to be no longer existent, never having cohered around any particular vision and thus not to be ranked as an enduring movement. The Diaspora, meanwhile, is assessed to be disconnected, divided, and lacking any real support base inside Iran. These views, however, are not based on solid evidence; they are more in the nature of a collective assumption.

There is a certain paradox in acknowledging the strong disaffection of the Iranian people while simultaneously dismissing all of the current opposition groups as not having any meaningful support. Other explanations appear more plausible. First, there is the intimidation effect of the regime's enormous level of repression. To express support for an opposition group means, literally, to risk prison, serious penalties to family members, and even execution. Even outside Iran, consequences had to be feared. Until recently, for example, expressing any sympathy for the MEK – a designated terrorist group until 2012 – would have made it impossible to obtain a visa to the United States. Thus the observation of the U.S. State Department's Iran Watch offices that their Iranian interviewees disavowed the MEK does not have much informational value. It will be more interesting to see if these statements remain the same now, after de-listing.

Even then, we are still left with the second explanation, put forward by Amir

Taheri and others. He sees the decades-long vacillation of Western governments as the principal deterrent to an effective opposition with public support. There is little confidence on the part of the Iranian people, he believes, that the U.S. will stand by pro-democratic reformers. Rather, the expectation is that the U.S. will sell them out in order to instead strike a deal with the regime. Many believe that the opposition is merely used by Western governments and particularly by the U.S. as a negotiating chip to be bargained away in exchange for concessions on the nuclear issue and that, in reality, the U.S. does not care about the rights or the suffering of the Iranian people. In this context, many Iranians view participation in the opposition as just too risky.

Partly because of this prevailing sense that the opposition is feckless, and partly because the Obama Administration does not wish to go too far in alienating the Iranian regime as it still hopes to negotiate with the regime over the nuclear issue, the Obama Administration cut funding in late 2009 for Iranian opposition groups, and the U.S. government – though still permitted to meet with members of the Iranian opposition – is no longer allowed to officially lend support to any such groups.

2.7: Conclusions

Upon reviewing the history of U.S.-Iranian relations since the Iranian Revolution, a few key themes stand out:

- *The cycle of U.S. policy follows a predictable hard-line to soft-line back and forth.*

The record shows that U.S. policy towards Iran has tended to swing back and forth between the same basic extremes. At times, the United States will grow frustrated with Iran and adopt a tougher line. This tougher line will manifest itself in economic pressure and beefed-up military assets in the region and, in the case of the Reagan Administration, even occasional military engagements. But following such periods of heightened tension, the United States will typically look for ways to dial back the pressure. In these periods, the U.S. presidents opt to make conciliatory public statements and seek to build good will through diplomatic exchanges around whatever policy issues are on the table at that particular point in time. Indeed, each new administration has swung back or forth in this way – from a conciliatory Carter to a more hard-line Reagan to a thwarted effort by Bush to enhance goodwill to a ratcheting up of pressure under Clinton's first term to a renewed attempt at outreach during Clinton's second term, back to pressure under Bush, and then back to diplomacy under Obama. The pendulum swings back and forth with almost mechanical regularity – but without much steady progress to show for either set of policies. However, the core of U.S. policy, beyond tactical and rhetorical ups and downs, has generally aimed at influencing the regime's behavior rather than siding with Iranians who are calling for regime change.

- *Even within the hard-line and soft-line policy sets, there is a surprising amount of redundancy.*

The hard-line and soft-line policies that have been pursued over time by the various administrations have also been strikingly predictable. Under the hard-line rubric, U.S. administrations have tended to consider sanctions on Iranian exports, freezes of Iranian financial assets, military mobilizations in the surrounding region, and UN Security Council condemnations. The soft-line policies, meanwhile, always tend to consist of presidential statements about "turning a corner" or "beginning a new chapter based on mutual respect," and other such pronouncements. These are then followed by attempts at conducting low-level diplomacy around specific issues – such as hostages, nuclear weapons, or other sources of tension.

- *Outreach attempts tend to be thwarted – either by events or by an inability to deliver.*

These various attempts at building trust and making progress on manageable sets of issues have not, historically, panned out. Events may interfere, as with the Iran-Iraq War and the Lebanon crisis under the Reagan Administration, or the killing of a hostage and the death of Khomeini under the George H. W. Bush Administration, or the uprisings and violent crackdowns under the Obama Administration. At other times, it becomes clear that the individuals with whom the United States is negotiating do not actually have the ability to deliver on their promises. Under Carter, this happened with the negotiated settlement that was agreed to by Iran's interim foreign minister in relation to the hostage crisis, only to be disavowed by Khomeini; it happened again with the "moderates" with whom Reagan dealt in the context of the Hezbollah hostages; and it also happened with Clinton under Khatami.

- *The constructive potential associated with the Iranian opposition, let alone the option of regime change, has never been seriously considered by the executive branch, and especially not under the Obama Administration.*

Although it is certainly possible – indeed likely – that different organs within the U.S. intelligence apparatus have secretly followed the path of various Iranian opposition groups and have even evaluated regime change options, no administration has explored this policy in any meaningful respect. Most administrations have instead taken the regime's existence for granted and have either sought to change the regime's behavior through various carrots and sticks, or sought to normalize relations through an incremental process of building confidence through low- and mid-level negotiations.

As a result, no meaningful outreach to the opposition has occurred either. The most serious work on this front was conducted by the George W. Bush Administration, which pushed Congress to appropriate substantial sums towards promoting democracy in Iran and which, at various times, spoke out in favor of opposition elements. But even the Bush Administration shied away from any specific endorsements of opposition groups for fear that those groups would be "tainted" as a result. This is an ongoing debate not just with regard to Iran but in the broader democratization and reform discussion, where some consider that fear to be misguided; reformers are "tainted" anyway, they believe, and should at least have the corresponding benefits of Western support.

3. Think Tank Views of U.S. Options

Against this backdrop of the various challenges facing Iran today, as well as the U.S. government's failure to make meaningful progress vis-à-vis Iran, the entire spectrum of U.S. think tanks and policy specialists has been very active in recommending policy options for the U.S. government's consideration. In general, we have found that the views among think tanks neatly fit their ideological leanings.

Figure 1: Think Tank views along a dove-hawk spectrum

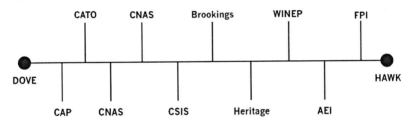

The more liberal think tanks on the "dove" end of the spectrum tend to favor further engagement with Iran. They believe that diplomacy (perhaps backed by sanctions) is the only way to solve our foreign policy dilemma vis-à-vis the country. If diplomacy fails, they believe that the United States should focus on containing a nuclear Iran. Some doves are uninterested in Iran's domestic affairs whereas others feel that the United States must begin to shine a brighter spotlight on the human rights abuses that take place within the country, as well as on the country's lack of freedom and democracy.

The more conservative think tanks on the "hawk" end of the spectrum, meanwhile, are of the view that sanctions are not working sufficiently either because they are still too weak and must be strengthened or because sanctions will never be effective enough to change the behavior of the Iranian regime. The latter think that military strikes may be justified. Among those who favor considering strikes, some believe in more limited strikes with the specific goal of preventing the regime from going nuclear. Others are of the view that regime change is the only option and that any strikes or other policies should be aimed at that outcome.

3.1: Continue with Diplomacy

Certain think tanks are adamant that the United States must continue to pursue diplomacy, no matter the cost. Perhaps the most prominent among these is the Center for American Progress ("CAP"). In an April 2012 report, several CAP scholars argued:

> We must avoid presenting ourselves with the false choice of either bombing Iran now or an Iran getting a bomb. The reality is that the Obama Administration's successful campaign to increase pressure on Iran on multiple fronts stands a good chance if its leaders realize the high costs of seeking nuclear weapons. [1]

CAP believes that the Obama Administration's outreach to Iran has "served as an important force multiplier for efforts to pressure the Iranian government"[2] by demonstrating that the United States is acting in good faith rather than simply looking for a convenient excuse to launch a military strike against Iran. The outreach has, according to CAP, enabled the United States to establish a multilateral consensus, making it difficult even for such countries as Russia and China to continue blocking the types of measures – such as tough sanctions – that would make diplomacy effective.

Indeed, the CAP report argued that the sanctions have been a helpful corollary to a policy of engagement, stating that "international sanctions and other measures appear to be seriously hindering Iran's ability to advance its nuclear research, thus delaying Iran's nuclear weapons ambitions."[3] They also argue that the sanctions have severely damaged the Iranian economy, constraining financial transactions and causing tankers to forgo Iranian oil.

CAP believes that over time, these various pressure tactics will force Iran to reach a negotiated solution with the United States. Such a course, CAP believes, is far more prudent than any military options that the United States might be considering as such options are a slippery slope towards an Iraq-style quagmire.

---

[1] See Rudy deLeon, Brian Katulis, and Peter Juul with Matt Duss and Ken Sofer, "Strengthening America's Options on Iran," *Center for American Progress*, April 2012, p. 1. <http://www.american-progress.org/issues/2012/04/pdf/iran_10questions.pdf>

[2] See "Strengthening America's Options on Iran," p. 3.

[3] See "Strengthening America's Options on Iran," p. 9.

According to Matthew Duss of CAP, the June 2013 presidential victory of Hassan Rouhani will not significantly alter Iran's goals of developing its nuclear program but further U.S.-led sanctions could still undermine any potential for closer U.S.-Iran engagement that might develop in the wake of the election.[4]

In April 2013, Duss published a follow-up article to the 2012 report entitled "Staying the Course on Diplomacy with Iran" in which he touts the "notable progress" made during the latest round of P5+1 talks on Iran and argues that "it's unclear whether applying more pressure can accomplish what a considerable amount of pressure has thus far failed to achieve."[5] Rouhani was critical of the way the Iranian negotiators have handled talks with the P5+1.[6] The article also asserts that the United States still has time to address the Iran crisis through diplomatic mechanisms, because it would take Iran "a year or more to build a nuclear weapon in the event that it chose to do so – which U.S. intelligence services believe it has not yet done."[7] The article's bottom line, then, is to keep pursuing diplomacy without further ratcheting up the pressure on Iran with sanctions or threats of military action.

Others have taken equally strong positions in support of continued diplomacy. Suzanne Maloney of the Brookings Institution, for example, believes that the sanctions currently imposed by the United States already constitute an overly aggressive policy towards Iran. She argues that the United States "cannot bargain with a country whose economy it is trying to disrupt and destroy."[8] For diplomacy to work, the United States would need to begin lifting sanctions to demonstrate good faith. Maloney believes that Iran would begin to take a more reasonable stance in its negotiations with the U.S. if it no longer felt that the United States was treating it as a threat and a pariah. The U.S. should, therefore,

---

[4] See Michael Duss, "Pragmatist Rouhani Wins. Now What?" *Center for American Progress*, June 17, 2013 <http://www.americanprogress.org/issues/security/news/2013/06/17/66820/pragmatist-Rouhani-wins-now-what/>

[5] See Matthew Duss "Staying the course on diplomacy with Iran," *Center for American Progress*, April 10, 2013 <http://www.americanprogress.org/issues/security/news/2013/04/10/60061/staying-the-course-on-diplomacy-with-iran/>

[6] See Duss, "Pragmatist Rouhani Wins. Now What?"

[7] See Duss "Staying the course on diplomacy with Iran"

[8] See Suzanne Maloney "Obama's Counterproductive New Iran Sanctions," *Foreign Affairs*, January 2012 <http://www.foreignaffairs.com/articles/137011/suzanne-maloney/obamas-counterproductive-new-iran-sanctions>

begin to taper off the sanctions that it has put in place against the Iranian regime and also soften its rhetoric so that the Iranian leadership can feel more comfortable negotiating with the U.S. government – and more confident that the U.S. is not motivated by a fundamental desire to harm the Iranian government.

Maloney has reiterated her call for a more diplomatic approach to Iran in the wake of the recent Iranian presidential elections. In her June 18, 2013 Congressional testimony,[9] she interpreted the victory of Rouhani as a success for the Obama Administration's strategy of balanced diplomacy. While acknowledging the institutional constraints of Iran's presidency, she nonetheless argued that Rouhani's victory represents "a significant turning point, albeit one whose proportions and precise vector remain uncertain."[10] Describing Rouhani as a pragmatic insider whose past political affiliations lie closer to Iran's traditional conservatives than the leftists, Maloney advocates a U.S. foreign policy strategy centered around significant sanctions relief in exchange for concessions on the nuclear issue.[11]

3.2: Prepare for Deterrence

Others, meanwhile, have taken the view that a nuclear-armed Iran is inevitable but also acceptable, and that the United States should stop devoting so much time and effort towards preventing an outcome it can live with.

The CATO Institute, for example, published a report bemoaning the "dismal record of sanctions"[12] in general. The report also explained that, with respect to Iran in particular, a policy of sanctions or any other kind of pressure tactic is bound to fail because there are so many other countries that have strong economic ties with Iran, including countries like Russia and China – countries over which the United States has little leverage.[13] These countries will never agree to robust sanctions, and thus will always dampen the impact of U.S. and European sanctions on Iran.

---

[9] See Suzanne Maloney, "Elections in Iran: The Regime Cementing Its Control," *The Brookings Institution*, June 18, 2013 <http://www.brookings.edu/research/testimony/2013/06/18-elections-iran-regime-cementing-control-maloney>

[10] See Maloney, "Elections in Iran: The Regime Cementing Its Control"

[11] See Maloney, "Elections in Iran: The Regime Cementing Its Control"

[12] See Ted Galen Carpenter, "Iran's Nuclear Program: America's Policy Options," *CATO Institute Policy Analysis* No. 578, September 20, 2006, p. 4 <http://www.cato.org/sites/cato.org/files/pubs/pdf/pa578.pdf>

[13] See Carpenter, "Iran's Nuclear Program: America's Policy Options," p. 4.

The report next evaluates a number of different policy options. Having already concluded that pressure tactics will be ineffective, it goes on to dismiss regime change as an option, stating that the risks are too high and that any "outspoken U.S. endorsements of [resistance groups] could be the kiss of death... [giving] the religious hierarchy the perfect pretext to portray even cautious advocates of political reform as traitors and American stooges."[14]

The only proper course, in CATO's view, would therefore be to allow Iran to go nuclear while putting in place a strong deterrent capability in the region. According to CATO, the United States has deterred other hostile regimes in the past, including the Soviet Union and North Korea. There is no reason to think that Iran would be any different.

Kenneth Waltz reached a similar conclusion, which he set forth in a *Foreign Affairs* article in summer 2012.[15] Waltz believes that allowing Iran to go nuclear will actually restore balance to the Middle East since Israel already has nuclear capabilities, which creates an imbalance that is dangerous in the context of an already combustible region. An Iran with nuclear weapons would lessen the chance of conventional armed conflict in the region since the risk of nuclear retaliation or other escalation towards nuclear war would be too great – a regional version of the Cold War's "balance of terror".

In one more example, in a recent report, the Carnegie Endowment also suggested that it may be time for the United States to accept the inevitability of a nuclear Iran.[16] In the words of the report's authors:

> Iran's nuclear program has deep roots. It cannot be 'ended'
> or 'bombed away.' It is entangled with too much pride—however
> misguided—and sunk costs. Given the country's indige-
> nous knowledge and expertise, the only long-term solution for
> assuring that Iran's nuclear program remains purely peaceful is to

---

[14] See Carpenter, "Iran's Nuclear Program: America's Policy Options," p. 7.

[15] See Kenneth Waltz, "Why Iran Should Get the Bomb," *Foreign Affairs*, August 2012 <http://www.foreignaffairs.com/articles/137731/kenneth-n-waltz/why-iran-should-get-the-bomb>

[16] See Ali Vaez and Kareem Sadjadpour , "Iran's Nuclear Odyssey: Costs and Risks," *Carnegie Endowment*, April 2013 <http://carnegieendowment.org/2013/04/02/iran-s-nuclear-odyssey-costs-and-risks/fvui#>

find a mutually agreeable diplomatic solution.[17]

The authors of the report go on to recommend a solution that allows Iran to have a nuclear capability with enrichment levels sufficient to enable power generation, but not sufficient to produce nuclear weapons. The report's authors believe that, given the positions (and various red lines) that the two sides have staked out, this is the only realistic solution to the problem at this stage. In testimony to the U.S. House of Representatives on June 18, 2013 and in the wake of the Iranian presidential elections,

Karim Sadjadpour of the Carnegie Endowment for International Peace was hesitant to equate Rouhani's victory to meaningful internal and external change in Iran.[18] He did advocate, however, further attempts to engage the new president and open avenues for dialogue. Citing the Obama Administration's success in building a "robust international coalition" against Iran, Sadjadpour advocates more creative thinking beyond economic sanctions to facilitate political change in Tehran.[19]

3.3: Focus on Human Rights

Several leading think tanks, scholars, and human rights organizations have bemoaned the fact that the United States is focused so singularly on the nuclear issue. These voices have argued that the United States would not only be more morally justified in focusing on human rights instead of national security, it would also garner greater sympathy for the United States with the Iran citizenry, thus further increasing domestic pressure on the Iranian regime. Thus, by focusing on human rights instead of nuclear weapons, the United States would be doing the right thing and would ultimately accomplish its strategic objectives more effectively as well.

The Center for New American Security ("CNAS"), for example, has argued that by focusing on human rights and universal freedoms, and reaching out directly to the Iranian public, the United States can make the Iranian regime feel

---

[17] See Vaez and Sadjadpour, "Iran's Nuclear Odyssey"

[18] See Karim Sadjadpour, "Realistic Expectations for Iran's New President," *Carnegie Endowment for International Peace*, June 18, 2013 <http://carnegieendowment.org/2013/06/18/elections-in-iran-regime-cementing-its-control/gaw7#>

[19] See Sadjadpour, "Realistic Expectations for Iran's New President"

weaker and more irrelevant.[20] CNAS believes that such a policy may even force Iran back to the bargaining table out of fear of losing legitimacy at home and abroad. Others have similarly argued that by constantly focusing on the nuclear issue, the United States is essentially fighting a public relations war on Iran's turf – the Iranian government can make a nationalistic argument for why it has a right to nuclear weapons, thereby stoking the national pride of the Iranian people and enhancing its own standing within the country. Conversely, it would be very difficult for the Iranian regime to publicly defend its human rights record, and a conversation about human rights would put the Iranian regime on the defensive. Experts from the Carnegie Endowment for International Peace have argued that a more representative, inclusive government in Iran would bring about greater political and social tolerance and that the U.S. should therefore pursue policies that restrict the Iranian government's control of news outlets, information, and communication.[21]

3.4: Ratchet up Sanctions

Still others believe that the key, at this point, is to ratchet up the sanctions, which are finally beginning to have an effect on the Iranian regime. The Center for Strategic and International Studies ("CSIS") is among the groups that make this argument.[22] In one report, it touted the impact of sanctions, which according to CSIS have begun to have teeth since 2011 and are now having a significant impact on the Iranian economy. In part, CSIS says, this is because the sanctions are finally multilateral.

Nevertheless, the authors of the CSIS report are not convinced that the regime has become fragile. They dismiss such claims as emanating from certain exile groups that have an ideological interest in presenting the Iranian regime as weak to further their own agendas. Hence, the report's authors do not believe it makes sense to ride the wave of sanctions towards a more comprehensive strategy of undermining the regime. Rather, they are of the view that the United States

---

[20] See Marc Lynch, "Upheaval: U.S. policy towards Iran in a changing Middle East," *Center for New American Security*, May 19, 2011 <http://www.cnas.org/upheaval>

[21] See Sadjadpour, "Realistic Expectations for Iran's New President"

[22] See Anthony Cordesman and Abdullah Tukan, "Options in dealing with Iran's nuclear program," *Center for Strategic and International Studies*, March 2010 <http://csis.org/publication/options-dealing-iran%E2%80%99-nuclear-program>

should continue to build upon the sanctions by further tightening them. They believe that, ultimately, the negative impact that the sanctions are having on the Iranian economy, including on government officials and other members of the Iranian elite, will drive the country back to the bargaining table and benefit U.S. negotiations.

3.5: Consider Limited Strikes

Some who believe that our current policy is failing propose putting the option of limited strikes of Iranian nuclear facilities on the table. Even CSIS, which in general supports a policy of continuing with sanctions, admits that if this policy fails, there must come a time when the United States considers limited strikes to buy the U.S. additional time before Iran goes nuclear.

One of the most vocal proponents of limited strikes has been Matthew Kroenig, who argued in a 2012 *Foreign Affairs* article that containing a nuclear Iran would be incredibly costly and would force the United States to make a series of risky security commitments to allies throughout the Middle East.[23] That price being unacceptable, Kroenig argues that the United States should seriously consider limited attacks on Iran's nuclear facilities. Kroenig thinks that merely putting the option of these strikes on the table, and credibly signaling this option to the Iranian government, may be intimidating enough to persuade the regime to seek a negotiated settlement with the United States. But if not, then a limited strike by the United States would set back the nuclear program sufficiently to make such a strike worthwhile and buy time for more diplomacy. The election of Rouhani to the presidential post in Iran likely will not significantly change U.S. strategy toward Iran, according to Kroenig, and the likelihood of diplomatic progress remains slim.[24] As the window for diplomatic progress closes, the Obama Administration's policy towards the Iranian nuclear program, according to Kroenig, will be "to prevent, not contain a nuclear Iran and (to ensure that) that all the options, including the use of force, are on the table to achieve that goal."[25]

---

[23] See Matthew Kroenig, "Time to attack Iran," *Foreign Affairs*, January 2012 <http://www.foreignaffairs.com/articles/136917/matthew-kroenig/time-to-attack-iran>

[24] See Matthew Kroenig, "Iran Diplomatic Window Rapidly Closing," *USA Today*, June 17, 2013 <http://www.usatoday.com/story/opinion/2013/06/17/iran-election-matthew-kroenig-editorials-debates/2432961/>

[25] See Kroenig, "Iran Diplomatic Window Rapidly Closing"

3.6: Destabilize the Regime

Finally, there are those who believe that the time has come for the United States to do whatever it can to destabilize the Iranian regime. Those in this group include scholars at the Washington Institute for Near East Policy ("WINEP") and the American Enterprise Institute ("AEI").

Scholars at these two think tanks have argued that the current U.S. approach is too focused on sanctions and diplomacy, neither of which has proven particularly effective. Although they admit that the sanctions have caused significant stress for Iran, they believe that to really have an impact, the United States must use all of its policy instruments to weaken the regime. This includes credible military threats, highlighting human rights abuses, and lending different types of assistance to the Iranian opposition. WINEP has explicitly stated that the United States should move additional naval assets to the Persian Gulf, and in regard to the opposition, it has argued that the United States should meet with opposition leaders, bring attention to their causes, and provide them various forms of technical support.[26] Experts from WINEP believe there is little reason to expect change in the Iranian regime's strategic objectives with Rouhani's win. Rouhani will likely attempt to reduce economic sanctions by pursuing greater transparency and increased interactions with the West,[27] but despite these projected overtures, will be unable to overcome the resistance of the IRGC and the hard-liners.

AEI scholars, meanwhile, have criticized U.S. defense planning for not devoting any meaningful planning resources towards looking into what it would take to effect regime change in Iran. They regard such analysis as necessary because "the Islamic Republic cannot reform and become a responsible member of the international community, because the ideology that defines its revolution places it in perpetual opposition to Western notions of liberal democracy."[28]

---

[26] See James Jeffrey and Thomas Pickering, "Year of Decision: U.S. Policy Toward Iran in 2013," *Washington Institute for Near East Policy*, February 12, 2013 <http://www.washingtoninstitute.org/policy-analysis/view/year-of-decision-u.s.-policy-toward-iran-in-2013>

[27] See Nima Gerami, "Nuclear Breakthrough Unlikely Under Rouhani," *Washington Institute for Near East Policy*, June 24, 2013 <http://www.washingtoninstitute.org/policy-analysis/view/nuclear-breakthrough-unlikely-under-rouhani>

[28] See Michael Rubin, "Iranian End Game," *American Enterprise Institute*, December 5, 2011 <http://www.aei.org/article/foreign-and-defense-policy/regional/middle-east-and-north-africa/iranian-end-game-the-us-must-settle-for-nothing-less-than-checkmate/>

These scholars maintain that through crippling sanctions, increasing our military presence in the Persian Gulf, and squeezing the Iranian regime using as many means as possible, the United States may be able to bring about regime change. This would be the most desirable outcome according to these scholars – and indeed the only outcome that would resolve the Iranian nuclear crisis once and for all. With Rouhani as the newly-elected president of Iran, AEI believes that Iran's foreign policy objectives will remain unchanged and advocates for U.S. engagement with Iranian dissident groups and labor unions as a way to achieve such regime change.[29]

Another think tank that represents the hawkish view towards Iran is the Foreign Policy Initiative ("FPI"). FPI's then-executive director Jamie Fly co-authored a *Foreign Affairs* article in 2012 arguing forcefully in favor of a series of military strikes on Iran with the aim of weakening the Iranian regime and creating an opening for opposition forces to topple the government.[30] The idea would be to hit the Revolutionary Guard as well as key intelligence assets, important telecommunications facilities, and various other tools that the regime uses to control and intimidate the Iranian people. Fly's view is that once the regime is weakened, the opposition will have the breathing space it needs to bring down the regime. The *Foreign Affairs* article stops short, however, of stating which opposition groups are strong enough to take advantage of the opening that such strikes would create, nor does the piece identify the prospective recipients and types of official U.S. support should the authors' proposed scenario materialize. FPI believes that, despite recent softer rhetoric to the contrary, Rouhani will pursue a nuclear-armed Iran. FPI reiterates that the U.S. should act swiftly to engage pro-democracy opposition groups while simultaneously pursuing military action against nuclear facilities and increase military presence in the Persian Gulf.[31]

---

[29] See Michael Rubin, "Iran's Moderate President?" *American Enterprise Institute*, June 17, 2013 <http://www.aei.org/article/foreign-and-defense-policy/regional/middle-east-and-north-africa/irans-moderate-president/>

[30] See Jamie M. Fly and Gary Schmitt, "The Case for Regime Change in Iran," *Foreign Affairs*, January 17, 2012 <http://www.foreignaffairs.com/articles/137038/jamie-m-fly-and-gary-schmitt/the-case-for-regime-change-in-iran>

[31] See Evan Moore, "FPI Bulletin: Rouhani's Win Distracts from Iran's Growing Nuclear Threat," *Foreign Policy Initiative*, June 19, 2013 <http://www.foreignpolicyi.org/content/fpi-bulletin-rouhani%E2%80%99s-win-distracts-iran%E2%80%99s-growing-nuclear-threat>

3.7: Put Various Other Options on the Table

Finally, there have been a few attempts at laying out a comprehensive set of options for the U.S. government's consideration without necessarily endorsing one option over another. For example, in the November 2012 issue of *Foreign Policy*, Stephen Hadley set forth a menu of eight options for dealing with Iran.[32] His recommendations ran the gamut from putting in place different types of interim agreements to buy additional time for a more comprehensive agreement (as well as to build confidence between the parties), to going straight for a grand bargain, to accepting the status quo, to also considering various mechanisms for ratcheting up diplomatic – and perhaps even military – pressure. Hadley's overview evaluates the pros and cons of each of these options without offering support for any in particular.

Similarly, RAND issued a report in 2011 offering a variety of policy choices for how the United States might deal with the challenges posed by the Iranian regime and its nuclear ambitions.[33] The report focuses mainly on how the United States might deter Iran from achieving a nuclear capability and discusses a range of carrots and sticks that the United States could use to change the Iranian regime's cost-benefit analysis of pursuing nuclear weapons. Among the sticks that the report mentions are various forms of conventional and unconventional military pressure, as well as more robust military sanctions.

However, neither these two reports nor any other "comprehensive" surveys of U.S. options give meaningful consideration to how the United States might work with the Iranian opposition as part of its policy towards Iran. This is surprising, especially in the case of the RAND report, which explicitly states that "Iran's leaders are . . . concerned about the United States using Iran's domestic opposition to destabilize the regime."[34] It would seem logical to follow that supporting the Iranian opposition could be another potential tool for the U.S. government in its dealings with Iran. And yet the report refrains from further exploring that avenue.

---

[32] See Stephen Hadley, "Eight Ways to Deal with Iran," *Foreign Policy*, September 2012 <http://www.foreignpolicy.com/articles/2012/09/26/eight_ways_to_deal_with_iran>

[33] See RAND, "Iran's Nuclear Future: Critical U.S. Policy Choices," 2011 <http://www.rand.org/content/dam/rand/pubs/monographs/2011/RAND_MG1087.pdf>

[34] See RAND, "Iran's Nuclear Future: Critical U.S. Policy Choices"

3.8: Reactions to Rouhani's Election

The reactions to Rouhani's election by most think tanks and scholars in some ways encapsulate the full spectrum of the views concerning how to deal with Iran. Many think tanks concluded that Rouhani's election presents an opportunity to reengage with Iran in a meaningful manner congruent with their prior position. Two scholars from the Center for American Progress, for example, noted that the United States should now "set out to work with the new Iranian president to see if a mutually agreeable compromise – one that recognizes Iran's nuclear rights and addresses the international community's concerns – is possible."[35] The Carnegie Endowment, meanwhile, argued that Rouhani's long-standing friendship with Ayatollah Khamenei suggests a level of trust that could "make him an effective interlocutor" and concluded that real U.S.-Iranian negotiations are now a more realistic possibility than they have been in many years. The Center for New American Security's Colin Kahl expressed concern that a great opportunity for reengagement could be squandered if narratives depicting Rouhani as a "more pleasant face of an evil regime" take hold.[36]

The more hawkish think tanks showed a greater degree of skepticism and questioned whether this development truly represents a broader shift in the dynamics of the situation. Foreign Policy Initiative's Evan Moore doubts the newly-elected president is a "harbinger of meaningful reform" and criticizes the Obama Administration for ignoring the reality that Iran has "pocketed concessions without reciprocating in kind."[37] The American Enterprise Institute's Will Fulton believes that Rouhani's election is largely irrelevant, as his actions will be dictated entirely by Khamenei.[38] But even these more hawkish think tanks have not provided further guidance on how to engage the regime's opposition.

---

[35] See Matthew Duss and Lawrence Kolb, "All in Moderation: The U.S., Iran, and the Way Forward," *Bulletin of the Atomic Scientists*, August 6, 2013 <http://thebulletin.org/all-moderation-us-iran-and-way-forward>

[36] See Colin H. Kahl and Alireza Nader, "Before Piling on New Sanctions, Give Rouhani a Chance," *Al-Monitor*, June 26, 2013 <http://www.al-monitor.com/pulse/originals/2013/06/us-ease-iran-sanctions-hassan-rouhani.html>

[37] See Evan Moore, "FPI Bulletin: Rouhani's Win Distracts from Iran's Growing Nuclear Threat," Foreign Policy Initiative, June 19, 2013 < http://www.foreignpolicyi.org/content/fpi-bulletin-rouhani%E2%80%99s-win-distractsiran%E2%80%99s-growing-nuclear-threat>

[38] See Will Fulton, "Rouhani Feels Limits of Office," American Enterprise Institute, August 2, 2013 <http://www.aei.org/article/foreign-and-defense-policy/regional/middle-east-and-north-africa/rouhani-feels-limits-of-office/>

Despite the range of views that exist among U.S. think tanks, then, it is clear that only a small number of think tanks have proven willing to contemplate meaningful support for Iranian opposition groups. And even those think tanks tend to discuss the idea at a fairly abstract level, mentioning that opposition groups exist and stating that the U.S. should consider offering them more meaningful forms of support but without significant analysis of who these opposition groups are, what capabilities they have, and which ones would be worthy of U.S. support and what might be the expected outcome of serious support.

Part II

Iranian Opposition

The Iranian government has repeatedly – and particularly at times of internal political crisis – accused the United States of actively supporting various opposition groups in Iran. These claims, however, have largely been self-serving, intended by the regime to smear any groups that oppose the Iranian government by linking them to ostensible U.S. government support. Conversely, certain opposition groups, including the monarchists, who are led by the son of the late shah, have at times overstated their own closeness to the U.S. government in an effort to bolster their credibility among the Iranian Diaspora.

The reality is that the United States has not had a policy of regime change or even regime transformation in Iran, and as a result, its actions to support various opposition groups have not been particularly robust. To the contrary, U.S. administrations have sometimes gone out of their way to make the opposition's life more difficult – as when the Clinton Administration, for example, designated the MEK an FTO, a move that was part of a broader strategic decision by the United States to achieve friendly relations with the Iranian regime rather than to support change via the regime's opposition. We could find no evidence that the option had been given serious review and then had been rejected; rather, it seems to have been dismissed out of hand. This is reflected in the generally poor level of knowledge and information about opposition figures and groups.

As noted in earlier sections of this report, the most aggressive efforts to support critics of the regime occurred under the President Bush, who sought and obtained funding for a Democracy Fund to bolster Iranian NGOs, put in place a new radio station to broadcast into Iran, and even met privately with two Iranian oppositionists – Reza Pahlavi and Amir Abbas Fakhravar. But even these tentative efforts were gutted by the Obama Administration, which dismantled the Iran Democracy Fund.[1] The Obama Administration opted for a muted response to the mass protests following the 2009 Iranian presidential election and the violent crackdown that ensued. According to a report, the President did not authorize any contact with the leadership of the Green Movement through the summer and fall of 2009.[2]

Within the U.S. foreign policy establishment – but not yet within the Administration – there has been a greater willingness to explore and support regime change scenarios for Iran over the past three years. As noted in the previous section on the think tank views of Iran, certain think tanks and scholars have come around to the idea that it may be time for the United States to consider regime change options, including support for the opposition. One of the policy options in The Brookings Institution June 2009 report, "Which Path to Persia?" was "to overthrow the clerical regime in Tehran and see it replaced, hopefully, by one whose views would be more compatible with U.S. interests in the region."[3] The study acknowledged that "Because popular revolutions are so rare and unpredictable, and because the Iranian regime vigilantly guards against any popular revolt, it is impossible to know how long it would take for the United States to promote a revolution in Tehran."[4]

Richard Haass, president of the Council on Foreign Relations and a self-defined "card-carrying realist," wrote in 2010 that he had originally agreed with the Obama Administration's reliance on diplomacy and negotiations to engage Iran

---

[1] See "US Cuts Funding to Iran Opposition," *BBC News*, October 20, 2009 <http://news.bbc.co.uk/2/hi/8315120.stm>

[2] See Michael Ledeen, "Obama Administration Ignored Iranian Opposition's Advice," *PJ Media*, February 27, 2012 <http://pjmedia.com/michaelledeen/2012/02/27/obama-administration-ignored-iranian-oppositions-advice/>

[3] See Kenneth M. Pollack et al., Which Path to Persia? Options for a New American Strategy Toward Iran," Analysis Paper No. 20, *The Saban Center for Middle East Policy*, June 2009 <http://www.brookings.edu/~/media/research/files/papers/2009/6/iran%20strategy/06_iran_strategy.pdf> p. 144.

[4] See Kenneth Pollack et al., "Which Path to Persia? Options for a New American Strategy Toward Iran," p. 103-120.

and a more robust sanctions regime if diplomacy failed, but now has changed his mind. Noting that the nuclear talks were going nowhere and the Iranians appeared intent on developing the means to produce a nuclear weapon, Haass concluded that the United States, European governments, and others should shift their Iran policy toward increasing the prospects for political change.[5] Reuel Marc Gerecht and Mark Dubowitz of the Foundation for the Defense of Democracies argued that the United States should pursue sanctions that lead to regime change. According to them, through sanctions, "a democratic counterrevolution in Persia might be reborn. A democratic Iran might keep the bomb that Khamenei built. But the U.S., Israel, Europe, and probably most of the Arab world would likely live with it without that much fear."[6]

The strongest support for the Iranian opposition has come from sectors of the U.S. Congress. This support dates back as far as 1992 when 219 U.S. Representatives issued a joint declaration in support of Iranian opposition groups, which read in part, "Experience has shown that this resistance's profound popular and religious roots within Iran's people are the best impediment to the Iranian regime's abuse of popular religious sentiments. Hence, this resistance is the solution to the phenomenon of fanatic fundamentalism. We are convinced that support for the National Council of Resistance will contribute to the achievement of peace and stability for all the countries in the region." The trend of support has strengthened over the past two decades.

Recently, the Iran Democracy Transition Act (S. 3008), introduced in 2010 by Senators John Cornyn (R-TX) and Sam Brownback (R-KS), authorized the President to support a transition to a freely elected democratic government in Iran by providing eligible Iranian democratic opposition organizations with assistance for the communication and dissemination of accurate and independent information to the Iranian people through various media. The bill attracted twenty co-spon-

---

[5] See Richard Haass, "Enough Is Enough," *Newsweek*, January 22, 2010, at <http://www.cfr.org/iran/enough-enough/p21293> By 2012, however, Haass had concluded that no policy can assuredly bring about regime change in Iran and recommended a course of strengthened economic sanctions: See "Haass: Answering Iran," Project Syndicate, January 27, 2012, at <http://globalpublicsquare.blogs.cnn.com/2012/01/27/haass-answering-iran/>

[6] See Reuel Marc Gerecht and Mark Dubowitz, "Economic Regime-Change Can Stop Iran Bomb," *Bloomberg News*, January 16, 2012 <http://www.bloomberg.com/news/2012-01-17/economic-regime-change-can-stop-iran-commentary-by-gerecht-and-dubowitz.html>

sors, all Republicans, but died in committee.[7] In general, Congress has been considerably more forward-leaning on the issue of Iran than other parts of the U.S. government, as reflected in their tougher stance on sanctions.

As previously noted, the think tank recommendations have not delved deeply into who the different opposition groups are and which might warrant supporting. If any efforts towards supporting the opposition are to be successful, a thorough overview of the opposition's make-up is necessary. This is also highly advisable for the contingency – which cannot be ruled out especially in light of the dramatic and largely unforeseen changes sweeping over the region more broadly – that political upheaval in Iran occurs without U.S. involvement. As the Syrian and Libyan cases tragically illustrate, Western ignorance about local political actors, factions, capabilities, and goals carry the price of chaos and a potentially disastrous paralysis.

This report takes the position that the time has come for the U.S. government – notably the executive branch agencies – to develop a more robust understanding of the opposition and to identify ways to work with the Iranian opposition to weaken, transform and ideally replace the Iranian regime. We reach this conclusion for several reasons.

First, the reality – as illustrated in preceding sections – is that the United States has tried every combination of carrots and sticks to induce the Iranian government to alter its behavior. The United States has been through periods of sanctions, periods of intense outreach, military threats, and diplomatic engagement. But throughout all of this, the Iranian regime has steadfastly continued on a path that is hostile to the interests of the United States and its allies. There have been episodic changes in tone, usually when heightened levels of U.S. impatience made it seem advisable to ratchet down tension by pushing forward a person who seemed to be a "moderate" with whom "dialogue" would be possible, but the objective record shows that these were purely cosmetic actions with no substantive outcomes. The reasonable inference is that the United States simply cannot put in place a more advantageous relationship with the Iranian regime as currently structured. Whether the current round of negotiation with the most recent moderate will have a different and more lasting conclusion is unknown, but the historic record indicates that it will be judicious to keep all options open.

---

[7] See U.S. Congress, "Iran Democratic Transition Act of 2010," <http://www.govtrack. us/congress/bills/111/s3008>

Second, the Iranian regime is quickly approaching a point where it will pose a far more dangerous threat to global stability than was previously the case. Iran is coming closer to achieving a nuclear weapons capability, which will drastically alter the power dynamics in the region. Once it has achieved its nuclear status, Iran will be able to threaten U.S. forces stationed in the Middle East and Central Asia, key U.S. allies in the region, and perhaps even U.S. allies in Europe. In addition to the direct threat that a nuclear-armed Iran would pose, there is also the risk that Iran would allow its nuclear technologies to fall into the hands of Iran-allied terrorist groups like Hezbollah. These dangers are too substantial for the United States to ignore, and too consequential for it to rely solely on the hope that "this time will be different" – past experience of U.S.-Iranian relations suggests that placing much trust in the intentions of the Islamic Republic is risky.

Third, the suffering of the Iranian people under this Iranian government has become a human rights calamity. Attempts by the Iranian people to assert their democratic rights in the context of the 2009 elections were brutally repressed, and as described above, the Iranian government still presides over an invasive police state in which the freedoms of the Iranian people are severely curtailed. Though accurate polling data is impossible to obtain given the degree to which Iranians fear publicly expressing discontent with their government, it is reasonable to infer that the Iranian regime does no longer enjoys substantial popular support within Iran. Unfortunately, there are no indications whatsoever that Rouhani intends to, or is able to, undertake human rights reforms. Persecutions and executions continue unabated. Regime opponents, including those with official refugee status and the nominal protection of the United Nations, have been repeatedly attacked and massacred even on foreign soil through assaults clearly traceable to Iranian official military organs.

Fourth, it is also important to note that, contrary to the common assumption and what Iran wants to portray, the current regime is facing serious crises and it is more vulnerable than is thought. The socio-economic problems of the regime, which have been referred to in previous sections, remain significant.

There are many important reasons why an attempt to achieve a policy change or a regime change through military intervention is neither attractive nor practical in the case of Iran. The country's territory is vaster than Iraq, and its population larger. The country's military capabilities are more advanced. In addition, given the history of U.S.-Iranian relations, a heavy-handed intervention would risk complicating the situation without resolving it. There are different views on the likely outcome of a military intervention. Some argue that it would stoke a nationalist backlash while others say it could trigger a move by the Iranian people to oust the regime. Without a credible and tangible Western policy of support for the opposition, however, the latter response appears unlikely. It further deserves mention that the American public is unlikely to support yet another military adventure, that world public opinion broadly assesses the two most recent U.S.-led interventions (Afghanistan and Iraq) as failures and other Western regime change efforts (Libya) as questionable in their outcome. And yet, most would agree that it would be equally perilous to allow inaction to encourage the growth of a hostile and aggressive actor, with a known proclivity for sponsoring extremism and fueling sectarian violence. What to do? What to do in particular if hopes for a diplomatic rapprochement are dashed?

This report proposes to add a factor to the equation: the Iranian opposition. It recommends that the United States develop an understanding of who the groups are, what they stand for, and what capabilities they have or could acquire, and that it begin to reach out to them in various ways that will be described in more detail below. Such an approach acknowledges the reality that the opposition can improve the prospects for bringing about an Iran that does not pose a threat to global stability or to its own people. This approach should be well-received by the Iranian people, who believe on the one hand that the U.S. policy of accommodating the current Iranian regime shows callous indifference to their suffering and is largely motivated by economic motives. It adequately reflects the recognition that a military attack against Iran would be going too far. A policy of engaging the Iranian opposition – made easier by the delisting of the MEK – however, strikes the right balance between prudence and action, between optimism and a naïve reliance on only one card.

4. Overview and Evaluation of the Opposition

Opposition to the Iranian regime commenced from the first moment in 1979. The coalition that ended the monarchy had assumed – and had been assured by the clerics and their coterie – that the religious contingent would withdraw from the political arena once the jointly desired change had been achieved. Over the years, the clerical leadership has proven adept at navigating periods of confusion and transition using a divide-and-conquer approach to split, weaken, intimidate, and ultimately dominate its rivals. Along with repression, a key item in the regime's armory has been its ability to divide its critics and opponents, put them at odds with each other, and sow dissension and distrust among and within their ranks. When combined with overt repression and suppression of dissident groups, it has proven quite effective. As the last and most determined opposition group, the MEK has borne the brunt of these hostilities. With some plausibility, its adherents see this as a measure of their effectiveness, arguing that the regime's measures indicate the level of the regime's concern with them and its determination to prevent others from rallying under its banner.

In the immediate aftermath of the revolution, Khomeini deliberately promoted a more moderate interpretation of its intentions.[1] Khomeini refrained from taking on all of his opponents at once, instead leading some to believe that they had a future in the post-Shah Iran. This tempted some groups to initially side with Khomeini. As described in an earlier section, Khomeini's first prime minister and foreign minister were in fact relatively moderate technocrats. But as Khomeini became more confident, he began to consolidate control. One by one, different groups were purged from Khomeini's coalition.

After June 1981 and with the start of mass executions, the political landscape changed drastically. The middle ground was gone and neutrality was no longer an option – one was "with the regime" or against it. For a range of reasons, the groups that opposed the regime did not easily find ways to work together to form a consolidated front against Khomeini. Many had longstanding rivalries

---

[1] During a visit to Neauphle le Chateau, while waiting for an audience with then-exiled Khomeini, we overheard his then-associate Bani Sadr instructing the team on how they should tell Western journalists what they wanted to hear in regard to human rights, women's rights and secular governance. See Cheryl Benard and Zalmay Khalilzad, *The Government of God*, Columbia University Press, New York 1983.

with each other and bitter ideological divides and initially were not sorry to see their enemies eliminated, realizing too late that the axe would eventually fall on them as well. Some groups opposed both the recently deposed Shah and Khomeini's new clerical-led establishment. Some doubted the longevity of the new regime, believing that it would soon prove incapable of governing; thus they hoped that their tenure as opposition parties would be brief and the important thing was to survive the period of ideological fervor and persecution. Instead, of course, Khomeini accumulated power and demonstrated the staying ability of his movement. He ruthlessly deployed that power against his opponents, which caused many groups to crumble as a direct result of repressive tactics or out of a realization that resistance was going to be a costly and long-term proposition that they could not sustain. The National Council of Resistance of Iran, formed by the MEK and its allies in 1981, remains the most long-lasting effort to form a coalition. The political history of the MEK and other opposition groups and affiliates is further expanded in Section 4.3 below.

The Iranian regime has continued to devote significant resources towards discrediting and dividing its critics – both inside Iran and among the Diaspora. The regime has pursued a concerted strategy to divide and cripple the opposition by combining outright suppression and persecution with financial incentives, including threats against family members' commercial interests in Iran.

Iran sows further discord among opposition groups by infiltrating them and the Iranian Diaspora in general.[2] The Ministry of Intelligence and Security acknowledges using a variety of tactics to infiltrate the opposition, including through identifying former members who still have ties to a group and can provide information; temporarily sending agents to prison so that they become known as activists opposed to the regime and then having them join established opposition groups; and otherwise releasing political prisoners (either undercover agents or real prisoners that have been turned) abroad.[3] Iran is also believed to have set up front organizations in Europe to recruit Iranian asylum seekers to spy on the Iranian Diaspora.[4] Reports of abductions, whether substantiated or not,

---

[2] See "Iran's Ministry of Intelligence and Security: A Profile, Federal Research Division," Library of Congress, December 2012. <http://ia601504.us.archive.org/31/items/IransMinistryOfIntelligence-AndSecurityAProfile/LOC-withdrawn-iran-rpt.pdf> p. 30.

[3] See "Iran's Ministry of Intelligence and Security: A Profile," p. 30.

[4] See "Iran's Ministry of Intelligence and Security: A Profile," p. 30.

are sufficient to create uncertainty and a reluctance to be too outspoken against the regime, even from the apparent safe distance of the Diaspora.[5] The security services of the Netherlands and Germany have reported MOIS agents working in Europe to infiltrate the rank of opposition.[6]

Over time, instead of a gradual normalization, the regime's human rights abuses have magnified, and the Iranian people have suffered through severe restrictions on their freedoms and endured the consequences of sanctions and of economic mismanagement as well as their country's diminished prestige in the international arena. Meanwhile, the opposition to the Iranian regime survived and intensified. Today, that opposition takes various forms both inside Iran and among Iran's vast Diaspora.

This report's recommendation, which we will detail in the concluding chapter, is to recognize the legitimacy of the opposition and meaningfully engage those groups that seek real democracy. We also recommend a unique strategy that we are terming an "additive opposition approach." This approach entails combining the strengths of different elements of the opposition, not necessarily in a coalition, but by helping to focus these groups' activities on their joint objective: real change in Iran.

Under this approach, rather than trying to reach a forced agreement on a shared platform and an institutionalized "united front," groups would clarify a shared goal, would then come to an understanding about their respective strengths and abilities, and would take on the tasks they are best suited for. To borrow a military analogy, instead of a united front, there would be joint forces in which each individual group would be comparable to an infantry, an air force, an artillery, a strategic communications unit, etc.

But before detailing this recommendation and explaining how the United States can act upon it, it is important to understand who the different groups and what their respective strengths and weaknesses are. To begin to lay out the framework for an empirical model that can guide an analytic effort to determine the potential for groups to bring about political change, it would be advisable to map the key elements and follow their track record over a period of time. The

---

[5] See "Iran's Ministry of Intelligence and Security: A Profile, " p. 30.
[6] See "European Intelligence Service's Report on Mullahs' Ministry of Intelligence," German security agency, the Office for the Protection of the Constitution, 2002 <http://www.ncr-iran.org/ it/guerra-psicologico-othermenu-53/servizi-segreti-europei-othermenu-54>

potential of the Iranian groups outlined detailed below have been assessed by taking account of the following measures of effectiveness:

1. Membership size
2. Target audiences
3. Support within Western governments and publics
4. Ability to disseminate information and messages into Iran
5. Ability to initiate or support political action in Iran
6. Information and knowledge about events in Iran
7. Ability to raise money and resources
8. Ability to build a cohesive political structure
9. Potential in Iran in a relatively free environment
10. Level of resolve and resiliency
11. Assessment by the Iranian regime itself of the threat they pose

4.1: Clerical Critics

Given that the current Iranian government is religiously defined and its core leadership legitimizes itself on the basis of their clerical credentials, the emergence of a deep ideological opposition to the regime's policies and even to its foundational principles such as *velayat-e-faqih* coming from within the ranks of respected clergy is extremely significant. Such opposition has the potential to affect the bedrock of the clerical regime and thereby to substantially strengthen the spine of the opposition. Therefore, while critics from within the religious ranks are not a cohesive "opposition group," the emergence of internal opposition within the clergy itself has a dramatic effect on the efforts of the opposition.

The clergy are powerful not just on the grounds of their moral authority, but also because they have access to an extensive network of religious organizations and societies such as the Coalition of Islamic Societies and the Militant Clergy Association (*"Jame'eh-ye Ruhaniyat-e Mobarez"*), which claims Supreme Leader Khamenei as its preeminent member. Within the clergy are hard-liners who resist any dialogue with the United States, oppose any form of liberalization, and are fully vested in the current system. This segment includes members of the Guardian Council, the IRGC, the Basij and the Judiciary.[7] They have

---

[7] See Saeed Rahnema and Haideh Moghissi., "Clerical Oligarchy and the question of 'democracy' in Iran," *Monthly Review*, Vol. 52, No. 10, March 2001, p. 28-40.

demonstrated a reliance on violence to eliminate, silence or demobilize political opponents.

This shared posture should not, however, distract from the very real and numerous fractures within and among even this segment of the establishment. While outside experts and observers are aware of the existence of significant differences of interest and ideology, as well as personal, economic and political rivalries within this segment, they have not tried hard enough to obtain a deeper and more fact-based understanding. They have not, to put it another way, developed an equivalent to Kremlinology, the Cold War effort to understand the Soviet ruling elites. This places limits on the Western understanding of the Iranian power structure, which in turn obviously limits the ability to identify and pursue policy options.

There are at least three different groups of clergy. One is the group that maintains total support of the regime. This group has influence because of its political closeness to Khamenei. The second are senior clergy who are religiously opposed to *velayat-e faqih* but remain silent due to risk-aversion. The third group consists of those who have openly criticized the regime.

Although the second group would no doubt serve as a resource on which to draw when momentum shifts against the regime, for now – because the group remains silent – its strength and numbers are hard to assess. However, the third group has been vocal enough that certain conclusions can be drawn. To be sure, these elements of the clerical establishment have gone even further than mere policy disagreements and at times even criticize the regime itself. The extent and persistence of this criticism is somewhat astonishing considering the level of effort that the regime has expended to control the clergy and the entire direction of permitted theological thought. Individual clerics and their opinions and associates are closely monitored; seminaries and curricula are overseen and carefully managed; and a combination of incentives and penalties has been imposed to ensure maximum compliance.

Nevertheless, these clerics have gradually come to disagree with the dominant political role the mullahs have arrogated to themselves. Some oppose the notion of a *velayat-e faqih* altogether on theological grounds, while many are apprehensive about the expanding disenchantment of the populace with the religious establishment. Some clerics had ties to Khomeini's former heir apparent, Grand

Ayatollah Ali Montazeri, and believe that Islam supports the principles of popular sovereignty and democratic representation.[8] Montazeri was once considered to be, religiously, one of the highest-ranking ayatollahs in Iran and successor to Khomeini. However, although Montazeri aligned himself with Khomeini on many domestic and foreign policies, he protested the massacre of political prisoners in 1988 and denounced the attempted elimination of the MEK. As a result, he was dismissed as Khomeini's successor.

In addition to Montazeri, a number of senior clerics criticized the government's handling of the 2009 election. These included some very respected within the establishment, illustrious personalities such as Ayatollah Sayyed Jalaloddin Taheri, a former leader of the Friday prayers in Isfahan; Grand Ayatollah Asadollah Bayat Zanjani, a senior member of the Association of Militant Clerics ("AMC"), which backed Mousavi in the election; Ayatollah Sayyed Hossein Mousavi Tabrizi, who was Chief Prosecutor under Khomeini; Grand Ayatollah Abdolkarim Mousavi Ardabili, former Chief Justice; Grand Ayatollah Yousef Saanei, former prosecutor of Iran; Grand Ayatollah Lotfollah Safi Golpayegani, a conservative who was the first Secretary-General of the Council of Guardians; and Khomeini's grandson, Seyed Hassan Khomeini, among others.[9]

A clear indication of disaffection within the clerical establishment was the statement by a prominent clerical group, the Association of Researchers and Teachers of Qom, in July 2009 that called the disputed election and the government illegitimate.[10] Along with the clerics, the religiously observant public too is showing clear signs of discontent with the regime. Celebrations during Ashura, a major holy day of mourning in Shi'ite Islam, in December 2009 turned into violent demonstrations of discontent with protesters chanting anti-government slogans. Security forces were reported to have lost control of some areas in Teh-

---

[8] See Ray Takeyh "Iran at a Cross Roads," *Middle East Journal*, Vol. 57, No. 1, Winter 2003, p. 42-56.

[9] See Muhammad Sahimi, "The Widening Divide Among Iran's Clerics," PBS, July 6, 2009 <http://www.pbs.org/wgbh/pages/frontline/tehranbureau/2009/07/the-widening-divide-among-irans-clerics.html>

[10] See Michael Slackman and Nazila Fatih, "Clerical Leaders Defy Ayatollah on Iran Election," *New York Times*, July 4, 2009 <http://www.nytimes.com/2009/07/05/world/middleeast/05iran.html?hp>

ran where they were met with fierce resistance by opposition supporters.[11]

Divisions within the clerical establishment were increasingly manifested in the run-up to the June 2013 presidential election. Vocal opposition to Ayatollah Khamenei transformed a several-thousand person funeral procession for Ayatollah Jalaluddin Taheri – the former prayer leader of Isfahan and dissident cleric who died on June 2, 2013 – into a protest against the Iranian regime.[12]

As with other actual or potential opposition sectors, the Iranian regime has moved to suppress clerical criticism. Montazeri was placed under house arrest, where he remained until his death in December 2009.

In the post-election crackdown, the websites of three senior clerics, Ayatollah Yusef Sanei, Ayatollah Bayat Zanjani, and Ayatollah Ali Mohammad Dastgheyb, a member of the Assembly of Experts, were reportedly blocked.[13] In February 2013, the intelligence services arrested Ahmad Qabanji, a Shi'ite cleric in Qom, originally from Iraq, and proponent of "civil Islam." Qabanj opposes religious interference in politics, supports the establishment of a civil state and fervently disapproves of the theory of the Guardianship of the Jurist.[14]

In addition to coercive instruments, the regime has numerous mechanisms to keep the religious establishment in line. Most clerics receive financial support through institutions run by the state. The government controls foundations and Shi'ite financial networks and an array of institutions—seminaries, research institutes, community centers, and libraries—whose principal purpose is the propagation of an ideology favored by the regime. Well-connected clerics receive substantial financial benefits and are cut into lucrative business deals.[15] The combination of coercive measures to punish anti-regime behavior and perks and benefits to reward cooperation has for the moment silenced much of the clerical opposition that surfaced at the time of the 2009 election.

---

[11] See videos in "Iran: Even more footage, pictures from Ashura protests," *Los Angeles Times*, December 27, 2009 <latimesblogs.latimes.com/babylonbeyond/2009/12/iran-more-video-footage-from-protests-surface-2.html>

[12] See Robert Tait, "Iran Funeral Descends into anti-regime protest ahead of elections" *Telegraph*, June 5, 2013, <http://www.telegraph.co/uk/news/worldnews/middleeast/iran/>

[13] See "Senior Clerics' Websites Blocked in Iran," Progressive American-Iranian Committee, October 5, 2010 <http://www.iranian-americans.com/2010/10/2235.html>

[14] See "Controversial Iraqi Cleric Arrested in Iran," *Al Monitor*, February 22, 2013 <http://www.al-monitor.com/pulse/originals/2013/02/controversial-Shi'ite-arrested-iran.html#ixzz2Mt76FuqI>

[15] See Khalaji, "The Iranian Clergy's Silence"

Theological and ideological considerations aside, the clerical establishment in Iran also faces a tactical and strategic decision. Some clerics believe that the Islamic regime has overreached and that its direct exercise of political power, by alienating the population, has been harmful to them as a class and is even turning people against religion. They therefore see it as being in their self-interest, and their religious responsibility, to privately resist and publicly oppose the repressive measures and excessive political sway of the reigning mullahs. But others continue to see their collective and individual interests tied to the survival and prospering of the regime.

Some authors interpret the differences among the mullahs as evidence that there is a possibility of reform within the regime or that there are genuine reformists even among the ayatollahs, some of whom are consequently referred to as "progressive." But others argue that the emergence of such opposition within the clerical regime is not because some are moderate, reformist or progressive; rather, is the natural outcome of the regime becoming weaker, especially in light of the fact that the differences are now being aired in public. Khamenei is on record as warning all factions that their differences should not be made public, even calling such public disagreements treason. But his warning was disregarded. Rafsanjani's decision to enter the presidential race is another example: Khamenei did not want him to run, but he ignored the warning only to be banned subsequently, a move that forced the government to show its hand and subjected it to international criticism.

In addition, Khamenei also faces a lack of religious legitimacy. On theological issues, there are many clergy in Iran who are more knowledgeable than Khamenei. This has always been a serious problem for the system. For this reason, for many years Khamenei was called "Source of Emulation for Shi'ites outside Iran" as with the presence of so many ayatollahs he could not claim such a position inside Iran. The younger generation, among the clergy in particular, has serious differences with the establishment. This trend existed since the beginning of the revolution, and as a result a few dozen clergy were executed. It seems likely that they would become more vocal if they felt the opposition were gaining momentum and receiving international support.

In short, then, while the opposition elements within the clergy could present a powerful force for change, they are also constrained – mainly because of the close watch that the regime maintains on their activities. In addition, because the U.S. government still poorly understands the clerical establishment in Iran, much analytic work would need to be done before the United States could work effectively with this group.

4.2: Reformists

As previously noted, the Iranian political system allows a degree of controlled electoral competition. The Council of Guardians supervises all electoral proceedings, pre-screens candidates, and certifies election outcomes – only those who are deemed loyal to the established system are allowed to participate. Nevertheless, at least until 2009, presidential and parliamentary elections created opportunities for political competition among factions within the Iranian political establishment. These opportunities for political competition have given rise to a "reformist" camp that has at times put forward a vision for the country's future which, while not directly challenging the country's overall governing structure, still sets forth a somewhat different vision for Iran's future.

The term "reformist" in the contemporary Iranian context encompasses a range of political tendencies that advocate various degrees of greater freedom and political participation, some measure of social liberalization (for example in regard to regulated dress codes), freedom of the press, expanded participation by women in the public sphere, and the like. These notions generally adhere to more progressive interpretations of Islam, but without fundamentally challenging the basic premises or legitimacy of the regime. As we will see, these groups experience high vulnerability to control, intervention and interdiction by the governing mullahs. The reformist camp is associated with the Islamic Iran Participation Front ("IIPF"), Mohammad Khatami's political vehicle, and the political parties of former Prime Minister Mir Hossein Mousavi and former Parliamentary Speaker Mehdi Karroubi, who unsuccessfully contested the controversial 2009 presidential election and subsequently supported the Green Movement. Internal reformers vary in regard to how assertive they are prepared to be in their efforts. For example, a third candidate, Mohsen Rezai, the Secretary of the Expediency Council and former head of the Revolutionary Guards who is often described as a "pragmatic conservative," initially refused to acknowledge the official election result but withdrew his protest after the Supreme Leader declared the election legitimate.

However, many argue that internal factions of the regime inherently cannot be reformist unless they distance themselves from the concept of the *velayat-e faqih*. They argue that one cannot be a reformist and yet believe in the Islamic Republic's constitution, which recognizes absolute power for the Supreme Leader. Moreover, they argue that regardless of the personal views of any individual, the system of *velayat-e faqih* is incapable of reform. The experiences of the past three decades back up this argument. Most recently Mohammad Khatami, considered a reformist in the West, said, "There is a principle in the constitution called the principle of *velayat-e faqih* to which all of us are committed. If we take out this principle, what will be left is simply a religious opinion versus other religious opinions. The principle of *velayat-e faqih* exists and we all must believe in it."[16] Regarding the presidential election he further stated, "Whoever wants to work must do it in coordination with the Supreme Leader and the Leader wants him or at least not to be opposed to him… If I want to enter the election I have my own framework. Working within the framework of the system and its leadership is a working principle for me."[17]

There are also illegal but tolerated liberal Muslim groups. The Freedom Movement of Iran (*"Nehzat-e Azadi-e Iran"* or *"NAI"*) was formed in 1961 by Mehdi Bazargan, Yadollah Sahabi, and Ayatollah Mahmud Taleqani (who later distanced himself from the group due to the NAI's conciliatory approach toward the Shah). While the group did not engage in revolutionary activity before 1979, it joined the uprising against the Shah and after the Shah's fall, Ayatollah Khomeini asked Bazargan to head an interim government (Bazargan resigned after the occupation of the U.S. Embassy). The NAI participated in the 1980 parliamentary elections, but party members were disqualified from running in all subsequent presidential and parliamentary elections. Bazargan was disqualified from running for president in 1985, as was Ebrahim Yazdi, Foreign Minister in the Bazargan government and secretary-general of the NAI after Bazargan's death in 1997.

Nevertheless, the party continued its political activity and backed Khatami in his second presidential election in 2001. In the 2005 election, the group sup-

---

[16] See Saham News website, April 21, 2013
[17] See Saham News website, April 21, 2013

ported Mostafa Moeen who lost to Mahmoud Ahmadinejad. With Ahmadinejad's government, the pressures on the NAI increased, and the Ministry of Intelligence prevented the group from convening its congress and from holding other events and gatherings. In the 2009 elections, the group asked its supporters to vote either for Mehdi Karroubi or Mir Hossein Mousavi. In protests after the election, the NAI called the elections "stolen" and Ahmadinejad's new government "illegitimate."[18] In the government's crackdown, several members of the NAI were among those arrested.[19] The NAI was a respected movement in Iran particularly due to the respect that Bazargan personally had among the ordinary people and also among the younger generation and intellectuals. Though not a "revolutionary" and hence not the ideal model for the younger generation, he was nevertheless respected. The founders of the MEK (discussed and defined below) were originally the younger generation of the NAI.

However, after the demise of Bazargan, NAI has gradually lost its significance and, in recent years, has gradually faded away as a movement or structured political party. NAI Secretary General Ibrahim Yazdi, 82 years old, is no longer seriously involved in political affairs. Although they continue to exist as a tendency and are known mainly as religious-nationalists, they have no political activity.

It is hard to know how much the reformists can actually contribute to change in Iran. To date, the reformists have tended to disappoint, failing to deliver on their promises. Most Iran observers believe that the reformists are kept on a tight leash by the regime. They are permitted to offer a certain level of criticism of the regime as a way of "releasing steam" but in a controlled fashion. If the reformists ever tried to institute any serious changes, they would be reined in.

4.3: Opposition

The opposition consists of those Iranians who are altogether opposed to the country's system of government. Inevitably, this group must conduct the major-

---

[18] See "Nehzat-e Azadi-e Iran: The Freedom Movement of Iran," Princeton University Iran Data Portal, <http://www.princeton.edu/irandataportal/parties/nehzateazadi/The-FreedomMovement-Profile.pdf>

[19] See "Nehzat-e Azadi-e Iran: The Freedom Movement of Iran." Prominent members of the NAI include Ebrahim Yazdi, the secretary; Hashem Sabaghian, Minister of Interior in the interim government; Mohammad Tavassoli, mayor of Tehran during the interim government; and Gholam Abbas Tavassoli, a sociology professor of Tehran University.

ity of its activities underground or outside of Iran among the country's Diaspora. Indeed, in light of the extreme repression the regime has been prepared to exercise, it is difficult to assess the extent of support for various opposition groups inside Iran given the significant dangers associated with expressing support or even just interest and sympathy towards any opposition group. But there is no doubt that certain of the opposition groups that exist principally outside of Iran also enjoy support inside the country.

The Diaspora has a number of important resources that could give it political clout, but it also has a number of significant vulnerabilities. On the side of resources, its financial strength is worth noting; it also includes an exceptionally high percentage of educated persons and professionals. As is well described by Shirin Hakimzadeh in a report for the Migration Policy Institute, this is due to the specific mechanics of Iranian emigration in the modern era. She identifies three waves of migration, all of which preferentially affected the higher income, higher educated and professional class and the elite. When the Shah was overthrown, close to 100,000 students were abroad in Western Europe and the U.S.: many stayed where they were, and a considerable number were soon joined by their families. Also departing were "families closely associated with the monarchy as members of the government, military personnel or bankers. These royalist sympathizers fled during the early stages of the revolution, often with significant liquidated assets in hand."[20]

Besides students and persons close to the monarchy, members of some religious and ethnic minorities also felt it wise to depart, including Jews and Baha'is.

A next wave of emigration and flight occurred in the years following the revolution once the nature of the new regime became obvious and once the crackdowns began. This group consisted of liberals and leftists,[21] later supplemented by young men evading the draft into the Iran-Iraq war and families unwilling to endure the social and cultural restrictiveness now in place as well as

---

[20] See Shirin Hakimzadeh, "Iran: A Vast Diaspora Abroad and Millions of Refugees at Home," Migration Information Source, Migration Policy Institute, September 2006 <http://www.migrationinformation.org/feature/print.cfm?ID=424>

[21] These groups of people were mainly from Iran's middle class and left the country due to the regime's massive crackdown; the MEK reports that this included a large number of its sympathizers, which would help explain the relatively good financial circumstances of the group.

"large numbers of professionals, entrepreneurs, and academics."[22] According to some reports, within a short period of time, the country lost half of its university professors, a third of its doctors and dentists, and 40 billion dollars in capital.[23] This makes for an unusually affluent, educated and resourceful Diaspora. In short, a good representation of the Iranian middle class is now outside Iran. This is important since the middle class has been the driving force for almost all major developments in Iran in contemporary history.

But there are complications that limit the freedom of this Diaspora to act against the regime. Many of these families believed themselves to be leaving only temporarily, or lacked the time to liquidate their assets. Many Iranian entrepreneurs continue to do business with and in Iran, which the government at least partially encourages for its own obvious economic motives. This is a double-edged sword: business people and others travel in and out of Iran, bringing information and somewhat limiting the ability of the regime to be a closed authoritarian system. But with their interests at stake, these persons are limited in their independence. Their physical property and business interests inside Iran make them vulnerable: critics of the regime can expect to find themselves dispossessed of land and family holdings. For those who have business interests or remaining relatives requiring the ability to travel back and forth, any expression of disloyalty towards the regime is risky. There is also concern within the Diaspora community that agents of the regime keep watch over their conduct and report dissident activities and critical remarks.[24] It is therefore only those with pronounced political standpoints, or with no remaining interests within Iran, who are free to engage in activities overtly critical of the regime.

This segment of the Iranian Diaspora has used its assets to give voice to and support a variety of different opposition groups, including the development of

---

[22] See Hakimzadeh, "Iran: A Vast Diaspora Abroad and Millions of Refugees at Home," p. 3

[23] See Akbar E. Torbat, "The Brain Drain from Iran to the United States, *The Middle East Journal*, Vol. 56, No. 2, Spring 2002 <http://www.jstor.org/stable/4329755>, and "Educational, Professional, and Economic Status of Iranian Immigrants," *Iran International*, Nos. 48 & 49, September 2008 <http://iraninternationalmagazine.com/issue_48&49/text/educational/htm>.

[24] The website RoozOnline asserts that a number of dissidents resident in the West have received death threats. See "Reactivation of Iran's Dissident Assassinations Program," *RoozOnline* <http://www.roozonline.com/english/news3/newsitem/article/reactivation-of-irans-dissident-assassinations-program.html>

media that broadcast into Iran.[25] For a period, these radio and television stations were associated with high hopes as their seditious effect was vigorously denounced by Rafsanjani and others close to the regime, but these expectations have since been reduced. The government continues to confiscate satellite dishes and denounce both entertainment with political content and Turkish soap operas or other entertainment it considers immoral, but this has become an almost ritualized tug of war of the authorities versus everyone else.[26]

The Diaspora, however, has also seen the reconstituting of many of the political parties that were suppressed in Iran. The 2009 post-election crisis temporarily revitalized the hopes of the Iranian opposition abroad – as Khatami's election and the rise of Iranian blogging, respectively, had done earlier – but it also revealed deep divisions over ideology and tactics. Diversity has been helpful to the opposition's resiliency, but the lack of unified leadership or a shared agenda has also been a critical weakness, as has the long and complicated history of relations among the personalities and organizations involved.

Externally-based Iranian opposition groups extend across a broad political spectrum that includes Marxist, social democratic, liberal democratic, monarchist and ethnic minority groups. The expatriate opposition consists of established political parties varying in size and significance, as well as individual intellectuals with clusters of interested followers, informal networks and bloggers.

Considering the importance of Iran to U.S. international interests, and considering too that decades of attempts to shape, influence, negotiate with, and reach out to the Islamic regime have come to naught, it is surprising that U.S. think tanks and the USG have not over these many decades acquired better knowledge about the Iranian opposition: its composition, size, significance, goals and potential to transform the country.

We would put the opposition into six categories, which we will describe in detail in this chapter:

1. The MEK and the NCRI, and some smaller affiliated groups, who appear to be the best-organized and most well-funded segment of the op-

---

[25] See "Iranian TV from LA is a regime-change hotbed," *Los Angeles Times*, June 18, 2003 <http://articles.latimes.com/2003/jun/18/local/me-irantv18>

[26] See Golnaz Esfandiari, "Nothing Comes Between Iranians and their Satellite Dishes – Not Even the Police," *Persian Letters, RFE/RL*, March 13, 2012, http://www.rferl.org/content/Persian_letters_satellite_dishes_iran_police/24514665.html

position.

2.   Assorted monarchist groups, which rank clearly behind the MEK and the NCRI in terms of organization and funding.

3.   A variety of secondary groups, which enjoy pockets of support but lack structure and resources.

4.   Several convening groups, which are attempting to create a greater degree of coordination among the different segments of the opposition and appear to have some backing from Western institutions.

5.   Unaffiliated intellectuals, some of whom are located in think tanks, or work independently online, or are based at universities.

6.   Unaffiliated activists, most notable among whom are the residual elements of the Green Movement, but who also exist in other countries.

Mojahedin-e-Khalq ("MEK") and NCRI

The People's Mojahedin Organization of Iran is currently best known as *Mojahedin-e-Khalq*, which was the name preferentially used for them by the U.S. military when it was responsible for the safety of the group's members in Iraq. The MEK is the dominant group within the National Council of Resistance of Iran (NCRI). It is the largest and arguably the most determined of the political organizations opposed to the Iranian regime. Even some of their sternest critics acknowledge that whereas the regime has been able to eradicate or terrorize all the other groups that participated in the original revolution but then opposed the clerical seizing of power and the imposition of an Islamic republic, the MEK persisted in its opposition despite enormous losses and today is the "last group standing" of all the original activists.

As a side-note, their superior organizational abilities were quite evident in the course of our research. Their well-oiled outreach machinery was able to provide us with volumes of material – statements on a range of historic and current events issues by their leadership, documentaries, statistics, and interviews with members and former members and decision makers. They were accessible, unoffended by sharp questioning, and diverse in the types of persons that held responsible positions and were put forward to respond to us. By contrast, we had far greater difficulties obtaining answers and responses from the monarchists, who clearly had nothing to compare with the infrastructure and organization of the MEK. On the monarchist side, it was difficult to locate persons willing and in any notable way authorized to speak for this segment, to get information and to engage in a substantive discussion of their platform. Websites associated with the monarchist movement contained contradictory or very vague programmatic content (A more extensive discussion follows below).

History of the Group

The MEK was founded in the 1960s by a group of Iranian leftist intellectuals and professionals who were opposed to the rule of Shah Mohammad Reza Pahlavi. The group suffered significant persecution by the SAVAK, the Shah's secret police, gaining it the reputation of toughness and determination. It participated in the 1979 Iranian Revolution but opposed Ayatollah Khomeini when it became clear that his actual agenda was not to retire to Qom and return to the religious life but to impose an Islamic Republic and wield power. MEK leader Massoud Rajavi was initially a candidate in the January 1980 presidential election but was barred by Khomeini. The French daily newspaper *Le Monde* was of the view that Rajavi was otherwise likely to have made a strong showing in that election:

> According to diverse estimates, had Imam Khomeini not vetoed his candidacy in the presidential election last January, Mr. Rajavi would have gotten several million votes. He was, moreover, assured of the support of the religious and ethnic minorities - whose rights to equality and autonomy he defended - and a good part of the female vote, who seek emancipation, and the young, who totally reject the 'reactionary clergy...'[27]

In the summer of 1980, the MEK staged several rallies in Tehran drawing up to 150,000 people to hear Rajavi promise to carry on the opposition to Islamist domination. On June 25, 1980, Khomeini responded with a major statement against the MEK, claiming their activities would derail the revolution and brings

---

[27] See Eric Rouleau, "A report from Tehran", *Le Monde*, March 29 and June 14, 1980.

back U.S. domination.[28] At the time, the official MEK publication had a circulation of 500,000 making it the most widely dissemination publication in Iran. The struggle between the MEK and the Iranian regime reached a turning point on June 20, 1981. The MEK demonstrated against the regime's crackdown, calling for political freedom and the release of thousands of political prisoners:

> Vast crowds appeared in many cities. The Tehran demonstration drew as many as 500,000 determined participants. Warnings against demonstrators were constantly broadcast over the radio television network. Prominent clerics declared that demonstrators, irrespective of their age, would be treated as 'enemies of God' and, as such, would be executed on the spot. Hezbollahis were armed and trucked in to block off the major streets. Pasdars [Revolutionary Guards] were ordered to shoot. Fifty were killed, 200 injured, and 1,000 arrested in the vicinity of Tehran University alone. This surpassed most of the street crashes of the Islamic Revolution. The warden of Evin Prison announced with much fanfare that firing squads had executed 23 demonstrators, including a number of teenage girls. The reign of terror has begun.[29]

In 1981, when the mass execution of political prisoners started, the MEK rank and file split into four groups: One group went underground within Iran, the second group went to Kurdistan – outside the center's control at the time – a third group left Iran for abroad while members of the remaining batch were arrested, imprisoned and in many cases, executed. Thereafter, the MEK moved into armed opposition to Khomeini's Islamic Republic. The National Council of Resistance of Iran was founded by Masoud Rajavi in July 1981, while he was still in Iran. Abolhassan Banisadr, the first president of the new regime, was dismissed by Khomeini, and joined the NCRI. Subsequently, in July 1981, Rajavi and Banisadr, with the help of MEK supporters in the Iranian air force, fled Tehran for Paris on a military aircraft from a military air base in the heart of Tehran,

---

[28] See "Reality Check: Understanding the Mujahedin-e-Khalk," Near East Policy Research, <http://neareastpolicy.com/reality-check-understanding-the-mujahedin-e-khalq-2/>
[29] See Ervand Abrahamian, *The Iranian Mojahedin*, New Haven: Yale University Press, 1992, p. 218-219.

a fairly dramatic illustration of the seditious support they enjoyed at that time.

In 1986, the group was expelled from France by the Chirac government as part of a political deal with Iran to free French hostages held by Hezbollah in Lebanon.[30] The MEK urgently needed a new place of sanctuary and found it in Iraq, where it established bases near the Iranian border.[31] Another political shift allowed the group's leadership under Mrs. Rajavi to return to Paris. In yet another shift, a raid was conducted by French police in 2003 – authorized again by Chirac as French president – and a number of headquarters staff, including Mrs. Rajavi, were jailed. The group's members were later released again and allowed to return to their operating headquarters in the suburbs of Paris, and the allegations against the organization and its members were dismissed. These back-and-forth developments illustrate the practice of Western governments to use Iranian dissidents as a fungible bargaining tool in their relations with Tehran.

MEK Ideology

The MEK's initial ideology emerged from a new reading of Islam, studying Western schools of thought and an intellectual debate with Marxists. Its texts sometimes used Marxist terminology, which gave rise to the assertion by the Shah regime that it was a mixture of Islam and Marxism. As we have seen, this was a not atypical combination during the 1970s in Iran and elsewhere in the Greater Middle East, where an intensive intellectual search was underway to find a doctrine that reflected the urgent desire for social justice and societal transformation while still having roots in local culture and tradition. Of course, politically, it was also convenient for the Shah and its secret police to label the group as "Islamic Marxist" to tarnish the image of the group in a country with

---

[30] See Hichem Karoui, "Iskandar Safa and the French Hostage Scandal," *Middle East Intelligence Bulletin*, Vol. 4 No. 2, February 2002 <http://www.mafhoum.com/press3/90S24.htm>
[31] See "Mujahedin-e-Khalq Organization," Global Security <http://www.globalsecurity.org/military/world/para/MEK.htm>

high religious sentiment.[32] The traditional clerics also had personal interests to use such a label for the MEK. Today, the group describes itself as Islamic but laicist (favoring the separation of religion and the state) and as democratic.

Paying the Price of Opposition

Over the past three decades, the MEK and their families have been prime targets of regime suppression. MEK documents include a thick volume containing the names, photos and particulars of some 20,000 of its executed affiliates, arguably the lion's share of those executed by the mullahs. The MEK estimates that in total, some 120,000 of its members have been executed by the regime.

In the course of the anti-regime demonstrations in 2009, many MEK supporters were arrested, and some were later executed.[33] The official indictments that led to the executions of three MEK supporters in 2010 and 2011 – Messer Ali Saremi, Mohammad Ja'far Kazemi and Mohammad Ali Aghaei – contained no allegations of violent acts. Rather, they were accused of providing news and reports on the domestic situation for MEK TV, recruiting members, raising funds for the organization, and organizing anti-government protests.[34] In addition to those who were executed, others died due to mistreatment and lack of medical treatment in prison.[35] Currently another person, Gholamreza Khosravi

---

[32] In rejecting the assertion that its ideology was a mixture of Islam and Marxism, the MEK stresses deep philosophical differences with Marxism which makes it impossible to reconcile the two and the organization's opposition to the Soviet Union, especially its historical role in Iran in siding with the ruling power. In his book *The Center of the Universe, The Geopolitics of Iran,*
Graham E. Fuller notes that the Mojahedin's Islamic orientation was a major impediment to the Soviets' effort to influence them: "The Soviets in the past have also been interested in other leftist movements such as the Mojahedin Khalq ("The People's Holy Warriors") but had almost no success in establishing any influence over it because of that group's own suspicions of Moscow and its nominal commitment to Islam." Mr. Rajavi in 1979 and 1980 held sixteen weekly lectures in the Sharif University in Tehran about the philosophy of Islam in which he drew a demarcation both between Islam and Marxism, and with Khomeini's interpretation of Islam. According to *Le Monde,* "Some 10,000 people presented their admission cards to listen for three hours to the lectures [... and additionally] the courses [were] recorded on video cassettes and distributed in 35 cities. They [were] also published in paperback and sold by the hundreds of thousands of copies."

[33] "Iran: The Gathering Storm," British Parliamentary Committee for Iran Freedom, March 2010

[34] "Iran: The Gathering Storm"

[35] "Iranian Cancer Prisoner 'Died For Lack Of Care'," *Radio Farda,* March 31, 2011 <http://www.rferl.org/content/iran_cancer_prisoner_died_lack_of_care/3543164.html>

Savad-Jani is on death row for his financial contribution to MEK TV.[36]

The MEK has been the biggest thorn in the side of the regime. In his decree ordering the mass killings of 1988, Khomeini wrote, "As the treacherous *Monafeqhin* (MEK) do not believe in Islam…and as they are waging war on God…. it is decreed that those who are in prisons throughout the country and remain steadfast in their support for the *Monafeqhin* (MEK) are waging war on God and are condemned to execution."[37]

Terrorist Designation of the MEK

Like the French government, the U.S. government has at times used the MEK as a bargaining chip in its negotiations with the Iranian regime. The Tower Commission Report of 1987 notes that labeling the MEK as a terrorist group was one of the conditions set by the Iranian regime to release American hostages in Lebanon. The report cited a letter by Manouchehr Ghorbanifar, an Iranian go-between, to his U.S. counterpart as saying that one of the demands of the Iranian regime was the "(issuance) of an official announcement terming the *Mujahedin-e Khalq* Marxist and terrorist."[38] After this came to light, the Department of State reversed its position and opened dialogue with the MEK representative in Washington. This came to an abrupt end when Rafsanjani, at the time the powerful Speaker of Parliament, promised that "if the U.S. government were to restrain the activities of the anti-Khomeini People's Mujahedin, the Iranian government would end its support of terrorist groups in Lebanon."[39] Soon thereafter, the State Department official informed the Mujahedin's representatives that policy had changed and he was no longer permitted to meet and talk with the organization.[40]

---

[36] See "Death Sentences and Executions, 2011," Amnesty International, March 27, 2012 <http:// www.amnesty.org/en/library/info/ACT50/001/2012/en> Gholamreza Khosravi Savajani, an alleged supporter of the People's Mojahedin Organization of Iran (PMOI) was sentenced to death in late 2011 after being convicted of "*moharebeh*" (enmity against God) in connection with his alleged support to the pro-PMOI TV station *Sima-ye Azadi* (Voice of Freedom).

[37] State Television, Channel 2, 30 December 2009; also see "Iran: The Gathering Storm," a publication of British Parliamentary Committee for Iran Freedom, March 2010.

[38] *Tower Commission Report: the Full Text of the Presidential Special Review Board*, John Tower, Chairman, Edmund Muskie and Brent Scowcroft, members (New York: Bantam Books, 1987), p. 359-360.

[39] United Press International, April 20, 1987.

[40] "Democracy Betrayed," NCRI Foreign Affairs Committee, March 1995.

In October 1997, the MEK was designated as an FTO. As we pointed out, a senior administration official at the time acknowledged that this was a "goodwill gesture" toward the newly-elected "moderate" president.[41] According to *Newsweek*'s Michael Isikoff, summarizing a conversation with Martin Indyk, Assistant Secretary of State for Near East Affairs at the Department of State in 1997, there was "... White House interest in opening up a dialogue with the Iranian government. At the time, President Khatami had recently been elected and was seen as a moderate. Top administration officials saw cracking down on the [PMOI], which the Iranians had made clear they saw as a menace, as one way to do so."[42]

In 1999 the Department of State added the NCRI, as an alias of the MEK, to the terrorism designation. Asked why this happened after two years, Indyk said that "The Iranian government had brought this to our attention."[43]

What followed was a lengthy campaign on the part of the MEK and its supporters, backed by key figures in Congress and with advocacy work by retired U.S. military officers, senior former USG officials including those who formerly held counterterrorism portfolios, human rights lawyers and others who had direct knowledge of the MEK, to reverse the listing.[44] This process has been amply documented, as have the refutations of the original accusations against the MEK that had supported the designation in the first place; they do not need to be revisited here.

In 2010, the DC Federal Court of Appeals ordered the U.S. Secretary of State to review the designation of the MEK. When there was still no decision by June 2012, the same court weighed in on behalf of the MEK, setting a deadline for the State Department to either substantiate or drop the terrorism designation. Frances Townsend, former Assistant to President Bush on homeland security and counterterrorism, has provided candid background information:

---

[41] See Norman Kempster, "U.S. Designates 30 Groups as Terrorists," *Los Angeles Times*, October 9, 1997.

[42] See Michael Isikoff, "Ashcroft's Baghdad Connection," *Newsweek*, September 25, 2002, <http://www.newsweek.com/ashcrofts-baghdad-connection-145143>.

[43] See Jonathan Wright, "U.S. Extends Restrictions on Iranian Opposition," Reuters News (English), October 14, 1999.

[44] Twenty-three US military commander and senior former officials on national security related issues such as Director of F.B.I., Director of CIA, First Homeland Security Secretary, Chairman of the Joint Chief of Staff of the US Army, and the Attorney General filed an amicus brief in support of delisting the MEK. Source to be provided.

The listing of the PMOI or MEK began in the Clinton Administration under the delusion that such a goodwill gesture might be received and reciprocated. That thinking clearly failed. The subsequent Bush Administration could have delisted the PMOI. Let me put a sharper edge on why I think that did not happen and let us be honest. After 2003, we were in a very difficult fight in Iraq. We were losing our men and women in uniform and I can assure you, being in the administration, that that was a very painful reality. If there was anything you could do to save one American life or one soldier you would have done it. … If in the midst of that fight in Iraq we had delisted the MEK, there was fear that it could have provoked a reaction from Iran. Let's be honest about why we failed during the Bush Administration to delist. We were wrong… not just because it was an unjust thing not to delist PMOI; we were wrong because of Iran's reaction. What did they do as a result of our failure to delist the MEK? It would have been progress if they had done nothing but they didn't because the tyrannical regime in Iran believed that that failure to delist the PMOI was weakness not strength. We know how the tyrannical regime in Iran reacts to a perceived weakness. They became more aggressive and they permitted, encouraged and actually enabled the transfer of parts for electronically formed projectile weapons produced in Iran across the border into Iraq which killed our soldiers. So, they do not understand good will. Their response to goodwill is direct aggression against U.S. forces.[45]

MEK Strengths

The MEK has a number of specific strengths. First and foremost, it is extremely well-organized. The group has its political headquarters in Paris and, until recently, maintained a quasi-military operation in Iraq called Camp Ashraf. It has networks on the ground in Iran as well and a large number of supporters among the Iranian Diaspora who provide financial contributions to the organization. It has a clear leadership structure and specialized departments for public

---

[45] Francis Townsend, speaking at a conference, Paris, December 22, 2010.

relations, foreign affairs, media etc. No doubt this level of organization is the reason why the MEK, unlike many other opposition organizations, has managed to remain resilient and strong over the many years since the Iranian Revolution.

While some see the MEK as exclusive and even as sect-like, its proponents point to the fact that the NCRI is intended as an umbrella organization in which anyone who shares the broad basic platform is welcome. They assert that after the overthrow of the regime, a provisional government would be formed for a six-month transition period, to be followed by free elections. We are, obviously, unable to ascertain the sincerity of this plan; however, it is difficult to envision a post-regime-change scenario in which the MEK could dominate the entire country and its political process. Khomeini was able to do so because he possessed a nation-wide deeply rooted network of religious institutions and persons. The MEK has nothing comparable and would presumably have to compete for popular support just like everyone else.

Third, the organization is able to mobilize substantial support internationally. Its annual rally in Paris attracts thousands of participants every year, including major public figures. Its detractors explain this attendance through the financial incentives it alleges the participants receive and the expensive machinery of preparation (multiple bus convoys ferrying attendees from other European cities and countries, rent of a huge hall, perfect choreography of the day-long event and glamorous speakers) but even assuming this is correct, this hardly diminishes the impressiveness of the group's financial and logistical abilities, both of which are critical to effective political action. Moreover, it is unlikely that such large numbers of people would attend the rather exhausting day-long rally if they did not feel sincerely supportive of the group, or that all of the highly distinguished American and European dignitaries would compromise their reputations and subject themselves to the borderline slanderous vituperation of their critics if their support of the MEK cause were not sincerely meant. Given their biographies, positions and financial success in life, the accusation that all of these people can be bought for an airline ticket to Paris and a speaker's honorarium seems implausible.

In terms of diplomatic outreach, the group enjoys considerable support in the halls of the U.S. Congress as well as in the British Parliament, the European Parliament and within the ranks of the U.S. military and intelligence communities. The 2013 gathering of the organization in Paris, for example, was attended by five four-star U.S. generals (General Hugh Shelton, General James Jones, General James Conway, General Chuck Wald, General George Casey) and four of the colonels who were responsible for the protection of Camp Ashraf.

Fourth, the MEK's stated values are quite modern and liberal. In stark contrast to the Islamic Republic, for example, they place great emphasis on gender equality, and on this topic at least, their conduct matches their rhetoric. Women indeed play a significant role in the organization at virtually all levels, including, of course, the fact that both the MEK's Secretary General and NCRI president-elect are women. The organization supports full empowerment of women in Iran and has repeatedly decried the degree to which women are oppressed by the current regime. The MEK are also strongly supportive of democracy as well as freedom of expression and freedom of religion.

Fifth, the group has a number of capabilities – related especially to intelligence-gathering – that make it interesting from the standpoint of Western policy. In terms of placement and access, the group's focus has been on collecting intelligence on threats from the Iranian regime against the group. Additional collection requirements include divisions within the regime, the nuclear program, and Iranian activities abroad in places like Syria and Iraq. According to two U.S. military officers who worked with the MEK at Camp Ashraf, MEK intelligence was generally good and reliable regarding tactical issues. In at least some cases, the MEK provided timely and actionable intelligence regarding threats to the MEK and U.S. forces.[46] This suggests that, at a minimum, the MEK had good intelligence in the vicinity of Camp Ashraf and other parts of Iraq.

During Operation Iraqi Freedom, the MEK declared its neutrality and agreed to concentrate all of its forces, previously distributed among 12 military facilities, in one location at Camp Ashraf to avoid being confused with Iraqi forces. This was strategically helpful to the U.S. and Coalition effort. The MEK also provided operational information to U.S. forces after the invasion about terrorist operations by affiliates of the Iranian regime that was helpful in preventing attacks on U.S. convoys. After the fall of Saddam Hussein, the U.S. military was placed in charge of Ashraf, which now occupied a unique status. Its residents,

---

[46] See Interview with COL (ret) Wesley Martin, May 2013 and interview with BG (ret) David Phillips, May 2013.

who were not prisoners of war because they did not participate in the war, soon reached a cease fire agreement with coalition forces, but their position in the new Iraq was precarious because they had been in Iraq during the time of Saddam Hussein. The U.S. military gave them the status of protected persons and became the guarantors of their security in return for their voluntary disarmament.

Assessing the MEK on strategic intelligence (e.g., Iran's nuclear program) is more difficult as this intelligence is much more sensitive. It did reveal, in 2002, the existence of two Iranian nuclear facilities, Arak and Natanz, which the Iranian government had not previously declared to the IAEA, along with additional details of entities connected to the nuclear program.[47] The revelations forced Tehran to acknowledge the existence of these sites and in some cases to allow IAEA inspectors to visit them. President Bush, Vice President Dick Cheney and Secretary Rice have all acknowledged that the Iranian opposition informed the world of the regime's nuclear weapons program.[48] Overall, the tentative assessment is that the MEK had substantial intelligence collection capability against the Iranian regime, particularly the nuclear target, in the past and, at present, still maintains at least modest capability.

Other capabilities include television and radio stations that are based outside of Iran but broadcast into the country; a successful public relations department that has made significant inroads with politicians in the United States and Europe; and the ability to tap significant financial resources when necessary, due to its deep-pocketed support base among the Iranian Diaspora. MEK-run television stations have also hosted telethons, during which significant contributions are donated to the organization. From August 9 to 13, 2013, Iran National TV, an MEK-related program that operates on a 24-hour news cycle, broadcast 46 hours of fundraising in a span of four days during which $4,545,000 was collected. Thousands called from Iran and outside Iran contributing anywhere from

---

[47] See David Albright and Andrea Stricker, "Iran's Nuclear Program," *The Iran Primer: Power, Politics, and U.S. Power* (Washington, DC: U.S. Institute of Peace, 2010).

[48] See U.S. President George Bush, February 19, 2005, in an interview with *Le Figaro* French daily: "It was an Iranian group opposed to its government raised the alarm with the IAEA." Also see White House Briefing on March 10, 2003; White House Press Conference on March 16, 2005; *Los Angeles Times* on March 25, 2005.

$10 to $500,000.[49]

But the organization also has been a target of significant criticism. De-listing has made much of it moot; what remains is the issue of how much support the MEK actually enjoys in Iran. The U.S. State Department is of the view that the organization enjoys very little support within the country, citing as evidence that the organization is viewed as a cult and that a majority of Iranians remain resentful of the role played by the MEK during the Iran-Iraq war. The MEK insist that they enjoy significant support, and that their perceived lack of backing is the product of a concerted propaganda campaign on the part of the Iranian government and also reflects the fact that Iranians who do support the organization would not be willing to declare that support publicly because the punishments in Iran for supporting the MEK are very severe. The MEK also points to the arguably enormous propaganda effort continuously expended against them by the regime as indicative of their popular support and impact in Iran.

In terms of the accusation that the organization operates like a cult, there is no question that the MEK commands strong dedication to its cause and to the organization, perhaps to an extent that can strike observers as cult-like. However, no hard evidence has been found to support the claims, occasionally forwarded by their opponents, that members are forcibly prevented from leaving the group, involuntarily separated from spouses or children, physically abused or the like. A delegation of the European Parliament and the U.S. military investigated the claims and concluded that they were unfounded: the European Parliament's report uncovered falsified information traceable to the Iranian Ministry of Intelligence ("MOI").[50] Indeed, the accusations that the group operates like a cult represent a degree of confusion about the organization. The discipline and dedication shown by MEK members is more akin to what one might observe within

[49] See "Iranian Opposition Satellite TV Channel (INTV) Ends Four-Day Telethon with Significant Success," NCRI website, August 14, 2013 <http://www.ncr-iran.org/en/ncri-statements/iran-resistance/14357-iranian-opposition-satellite-tv-channel-intv-ends-4-day-telethon-with-significant-success>

[50] See Andre Brie, Paulo Casaca, Azadeh Zabeti, "People's Mojahedin of Iran – Mission Report," European Parliament, Friends of a Free Iran, L'Harmattan Publishers, September 2005. Regarding the U.S. military, which had control of Camp Ashraf and repeatedly entered the camp unannounced to conduct inspections and follow up on allegations, see Congressional Record-Extension of Remarks, June 21, 2005, p. E1299.

the ranks of a standard military organization – which, in Ashraf, they were.[51]

The Monarchists

It is worth noting at the outset that the term "monarchists" requires caveats. The most apt description for this group is that it encompasses those who support the royal family, and more specifically the former Crown Prince Reza Pahlavi in some form or fashion – but not necessarily in a monarchic capacity. It also includes persons who feel that Iran was a better country in the days before the Islamic Republic, and who view the monarchist era with some nostalgia as a time when the country was more secular and more oriented towards modernity.

Reza Pahlavi is the eldest son of the former Shah of Iran. He left Iran and came to the United States at the age of 17, just before the Iranian Revolution, to be trained as an air force pilot and study at Williams College and at the University of Southern California. After the fall of the monarchy, he remained in the United States and became a political voice within the Iranian Diaspora. He has published several books, including *Winds of Change*, which advocates democracy and human rights albeit in a rather general philosophical way.

Pahlavi's own views can be somewhat difficult to categorize. For example, in a recent interview with a Bahraini newspaper, he urged a "democratic transition," warned that if this was obstructed by the current regime he would instead call for an "ouster of the Islamic regime," and then – without explaining how the democratic transition might unfold or how such an ouster would occur – stated that when and if his supporters succeeded in effecting regime change, there would be a "transitional period" during which the population could decide if they wanted a "democratic republic or a monarchy."[52]

Pahlavi voiced his support for the aspirations of the Green Movement, and at other times has come out in favor of the empowerment of young Iranians. In this respect, he has had to straddle a fine line. Many of his supporters – in

---

[51] For more information on MEK members and their organization in Camp Ashraf, see Lincoln Bloomfield, Jr., *The Mujahedin-e Khalq: Shackled by a Twisted History*, Baltimore: University of Baltimore, 2013.

[52] See "Exclusive interview with the Bahraini daily newspaper Al-Bilad's Editor-in-Chief Munis Al-Mardi," *Bahrain News Agency*, May 2, 2013 <www.rezapahlavi.org/details_article.php? english&article=646>

particular those who back him financially – are more traditional monarchists and hence support the restoration of the monarchy in Iran. For these supporters, the expectation is that Pahlavi would restore the monarchy and become king if he returned to Iran. This may be his personal aspiration too, but he presumably knows that showing his hand at this point would significantly limit his popularity. Thus, at least publicly, Pahlavi has been careful to keep his plans ambiguous. However, he uses the title 'Prince' in official media statements and interviews, and his mother's website terms itself the "official website of the Empress Farah Diba."[53]

An example of a group that supports a constitutional monarchy with Pahlavi at its helm is the Constitutionalist Party of Iran ("CPI"). However, the party has declared itself willing to accept a republic if that should be the will of the Iranian people. It rejects both religious politics and the use of violence: its stated goal is to support the internal Iranian opposition and take advantage of what it believes to be the regime's weakening in order to bring it down without violence.[54] The CPI is based in Münster, Germany, and claims to have branches in Denmark, Sweden, Norway, the Netherlands, France, Belgium, the United Kingdom, Canada, and the United States. According to an assessment published by the Canadian Immigration and Refugee Board, the CPI presents no serious challenge to the Iranian government since its activities are limited to propaganda.[55] Some critics also point out that while the grim conditions imposed by the mullah regime make some Iranians retrospectively regard the era of the Shah's rule with nostalgia, many remember that it was the Shah's poor governance, disconnect from the popular will, inability to address the economic inequalities and backwardness, and repression of civil liberties that created the pre-revolutionary conditions in the first place.

Adherents of the CPI assert that they have sympathizers in high places within the regime – "sleepers" who are awaiting the signal to "turn." It is not possible to ascertain the correctness of this claim, and we were not presented with any

---

[53] See Official Website of the Empress Farah Pahlavi <http://www.farahpahlavi.org>

[54] See "The Constitutionalist Party of Iran (Liberal Democrats)," <http://www.irancpi.net/index.php>

[55] See Immigration and Refugee Board of Canada, "Iran: Treatment of members of the Constitutionalist Party of Iran (CPI or ICPI) by Iranian government agents," April 17, 2003 <http://www.refworld.org/cgi-bin/texis/vtx/rwmain?page=country&category=&publisher=IRBC&type=&coi=IRN&rid=&docid=3f7d4daf3&skip=0>

evidence to back it.

Pahlavi followers have recently created an entity called the NCI, an obvious intended rival to the MEK and the longstanding NCRI. According to its supporters the NCI is a coalition of "twelve Iranian nationalist parties" led by Pahlavi. Our research indicates that this, at least thus far, is at best a fledgling effort. The launch was sparsely attended and the two-day event, by member accounts, was dominated by procedural and political disagreements.

The monarchists include members of significant families, some with long and respected histories in Iran. To some strata of the population, they are a positive reminder of an era that, with its many problems, is also associated with greatness, elegance, high culture, modernization, and regional respect. They have financial assets and ongoing economic ties and activities through partners, relatives, and their own continued investments and companies in Iran. What they bring to the table is the support of a distinct demographic, a portion of the upper and upper middle classes; a number of educated and trained professionals, some of whom have strong sentimental and practical ties to Iran and would probably return if the circumstances allowed; and the capital and financial knowledge to help keep the economy going during a transition period and to invigorate it thereafter. The last point is likely to greatly ease the stabilization and state-building period.

This group, however, also has significant weaknesses and some of its strengths are double-edged. The average Iranian would likely not take kindly to the mass return of individuals and families who, having spent the dark decades elsewhere in comfort, are now back to reclaim their former positions of privilege. The monarchists cannot point to the same degree of sacrifice and determined struggle that some of the other opposition groups have endured. Their return could therefore look like opportunism. In addition, despite all the suffering under the clerical regime, there is no indication that there is any serious appetite in Iran for a return to a system of monarchy.

Also, the group remains factionalized and divided and does not seem to have made any noteworthy progress towards greater cohesiveness, better organization, effective outreach or tactical planning during the past years. It has a titular leader in the son of the former Shah, and to hardcore monarchist loyalists, he is a figure vested with enormous saliency. But there are others who regard him as not very relevant, some who favor a constitutional monarchy with a purely symbolic role for the king, and still others who decidedly oppose a return of the monarchy and at most would accept "citizen Reza" as an ordinary candidate for political office. There are also non-ideological divisions within the group of monarchists – personal, family, business, regional and other rivalries that cause disagreement and distrust. Participants relate that rivalries regularly ensue over the division of political offices for the distant post-regime future.

Accordingly, their biggest flaw is that they have not established any real structures to the point where it is questionable whether they are even properly a "group." There have been some meetings and congresses, but nothing like an effective, ongoing organization. Sporadically, efforts are made to remedy this. In 1994, a Constitutionalist Party was formed to support the creation of a constitutional monarchy in Iran; however, in the years since then, its members have not even managed to create a Wikipedia entry, and one finds only a placeholder consisting of three sentences. On April 29, 2013, at a gathering in Paris, the formation of a National Council of Iran was announced. Even the official online images of the event reveal its sparse attendance while the accompanying text reflects an absence of consensus, with some participants self-describing as "monarchists" and others as "social democrats." "Prince" Reza received the title of "spokesman" and the platform announced the "overthrow of the Iranian regime through civil disobedience," to be followed by a referendum.[56]

Secondary Groups

Next in the list come a handful of other groups that support varying ideologies. These groups exist in Canada, the United States, and Europe. They enjoy pockets of support. In the main, however, they are less organized and have less funding than the MEK or even the Monarchists.

The Organization of the Iranian People's Fedayeen

During the 1960s and 1970s, a number of mostly student-based associations and groups came into being as idealistic young people struggled to understand and seek ways to address the social, economic, and political inequities in their

---

[56] See Carl Melchers, "The First Gathering of the National Council of Iran in Paris," May 16, 2013 <http://allison4iran.blogspot.com/2013/05/first-gathering-of-national-council-of.html>

country. Typically, their ideological platforms and philosophical approaches represented a blend of various Communist ideas, and the groups generally became embroiled in disputes and factionalism – a phenomenon no different from what occurred in student and leftist circles in Western Europe, Russia, Eastern Europe, and Latin America. Communism, Maoism, Leninism, Stalinism, Trotsky, Che Guevara – all lent their respective inspiration and were applied in different ways to the young activists' thinking about how to bring real and fundamental change to Iran. Was armed struggle justified or not? Was reform possible or was a revolution required? Was the Soviet Union an inspiration or was it just as bad as the imperialists? Groups split and split again over such issues. The pattern carried over into the post-Shah period, and even after the religious government had embarked on its brutal persecution of leftists, some leftist groups still held that while the Islamic Republic was a negative and not what they had intended as the outcome of the revolution, it nonetheless held anti-imperialist values and therefore deserved temporarily to be supported in a common struggle against capitalism and the West.

For a prime example of this dynamic and its consequences, we can look to the Iranian Fedayeen, an organization founded in 1971 in opposition to the monarchy and also to the Tudeh Party, which in its view was a tool of the Soviet Union and had betrayed the true interests of the Iranian people and workers. Yassamine Mather, who identifies herself as a former member of the Fedayeen, offers a detailed description of the group's history, development and fatal flaws in her article "Learn the Lessons of the Fedayeen":

> [From] 1971-79 the organization was mainly underground, preparing for armed warfare and organizing the occasional bank robbery. Its activities were sporadic – the Fedayeen killed a couple of American military personnel in Teheran and a number of the Shah's generals...Many Fedayeen spent this period in prison.[57]

During this period and especially among the jailed leaders, ideological debate flourished and with it came schisms. Mather believes that while the Fedayeen collected many admirers among the students, the young, the intellectuals and

---

[57] See Yassamine Mather, "Learn the Lessons of the Fedayeen" <www.hopoi.org/fedayeen.html>

artists for their principled stand and obvious courage, they "had no strategy about what to do, now that the revolutionary situation had arrived. That was the problem of February 1979. While the clergy used the period of economic crisis (1974-79) to build their base, to make propaganda, taking advantage of their position in the mosque to organize and mobilize, the Fedayeen in prison were still debating in very abstract terms such questions as the united front against the dictatorship...It is not, therefore, a question of the February Revolution being hijacked: more the fact that the Left was simply not prepared for it."[58]

The 1979 revolution did, however, initially achieve the release of many political prisoners. Set free but disagreeing over the issue of armed struggle, the Fedayeen now split into a group calling itself the Fedayeen Majority and another calling itself the Fedayeen Minority. The Majority considered Bijan Jazani to be its intellectual leader[59], a man who had been condemned to life imprisonment and had spent eight years in prison when he was secretly put before a firing squad, along with six other Fedayeen members and two MEK members, on April 20, 1975. Subsequently, SAVAK claimed that they had been shot while attempting to escape. However, soon after the revolution the Majority shifted towards the Tudeh Party. The Majority supported the occupation of the U.S. embassy. The Minority did not, and they also opposed the Iran-Iraq war – two positions that put them at odds with the Islamic regime and caused them to be persecuted. The Fedayeen Majority at this point was still on good terms with the Islamic government, as was the Tudeh Party. With their situation no longer tenable inside Iran, the Minority moved to Kurdistan. There, over a period of years, the difficult environmental conditions and further rifts eventually led to additional splits within the group. Only one splinter group has remained active; today, it is a member of the NCRI and advocates a democratic and nationalist approach.

The Majority wing held on inside Iran into the mid 1980s. It called for a relationship of "critical unity" towards the Islamic Republic, which basically meant that it supported many of the regime's foreign policy positions but did not endorse a religious state. The group did, however, cooperate very closely

---

[58] See Mather, "Learn the Lessons of the Fedayeen," p. 2.

[59] It seems, however, that the Minority and indeed all splinters from the original Fedayeen revered Jazani, as did many non-Marxist Iranian intellectuals.

with the regime and even aided in the brutal crackdown on other opposition groups in the early 1980s. Many other opposition groups remain hostile to the Fedayeen for this reason. The government, however, was only waiting until it had sufficiently consolidated its hold and thereafter, it moved with great brutality against all remaining leftist forces including the Fedayeen Majority. Hundreds were jailed and some were killed, including key leaders; others were able to flee and reestablish themselves and the organization abroad. In 1990, a party Congress officially reversed course and declared its opposition to the Islamic Republic. Currently, its platform emphasizes secularism and democratic socialism and the group has undertaken some attempts to rejoin other small leftist associations. It also maintains ongoing relations with the Communist parties of several European states.[60]

The National Front of Iran

The National Front of Iran ("*Jebhe Melli*") traces its ancestry to a coalition of secular nationalist and social democratic groups that supported the Mossadegh government. In different configurations, it constituted the main opposition to the Pahlavi regime after the 1953 coup. Under Karim Sanjabi's leadership, the group reconstituted in 1977. Sanjabi was for a short period the foreign minister and the group also placed a few other ministers in the first government after the Revolution, but they soon came under attack by Khomeini, who accused the Front of apostasy for opposing the harsh Islamic penal code he favored. Sanjabi and others then went into exile.[61] After Sanjabi's death in 1995, the group was headed by the poet Adib Boroumand.[62] The National Front has branches in Europe and the United States. In the United States, the group has chapters in Chicago, New York, Los Angeles and Fairfax, Virginia.[63] However, the website of the group's leader states that NFI has no representative outside of Iran. It appears to have an aging membership with no new base of support.

---

[60] See "A Glance at the History of the Organization of Iranian People's Fadaian (Majority)," September 2007 <http://www.fadai.org/english/history-07.pdf>

[61] For the climactic confrontation between the Front and Khomeini see <www.youtube.com/watch?v=JkEcUjqUTlo>

[62] For Boroumand's website, see <http://www.adibboroumand.com/>

[63] See "Iranian National Front-USA," <http://jebhemelli.net/>

The Union for Democracy in Iran ("UDI")

Founded in Stockholm in February 2012 with assistance from the Olaf Palme Center, the UDI was designed to be a platform for building consensus among the different sectors of the Iranian opposition and achieving greater cooperation and coordination. The UDI held conferences in Brussels and Prague in 2012, attended by representatives of the smaller Iranian political tendencies abroad but not by the royalists, the MEK, or the radical wing of the Communist Party. The organizers include Mohsen Sazgara, one of the founders of the Revolutionary Guards and Deputy Prime Minister under Mousavi in the 1980s, in exile since 2004, and Javad Khadem, a close aide to assassinated former Prime Minister Shapour Bakhtiar.[64] UDI is not an organization or political party but consists of individuals with diverse and even opposing views and interests. They have no joint activities beyond occasional attendance at conferences. Following the Prague conference several participants disassociated themselves from the final declaration.

The Tudeh Party of Iran

The Tudeh (Communist) Party used to be an extremely important political force but is now largely defunct within Iran. Many members of the Central Committee and hundreds of cadres were executed in the 1980s. The key leaders of the group Noureddin Kianoori and Ehsan Tabari, the ideologue of the party, declared in prison that they had converted to Islam, and published books denouncing Marxism. Efforts were made to reconstruct the party outside Iran, but it currently has no effective structure. Ali Khavari, at 90 years old, has been First Secretary since 1985.

Jundullah (Army of God)

Jundullah is an ethnic Baluch Sunni Iranian armed group that has carried out attacks against Iranian state interests in Iranian Baluchistan, including an assassination attempt on President Ahmadinejad in 2005. The group's leader, Abdul Malik Rigi, was captured by Pakistani security forces and extradited to Iran,

---

[64] See "Des opposants en exil tentent de s'organiser," *Le Monde Proche-Orient*, December 7, 2012 <http://entekhabehazadenglish.wordpress.com/>

where he was executed in June 2010.[65] Jundullah was placed on the U.S. FTO list in November 2010 on the grounds that its attacks had targeted civilians. Some analysts viewed the designation as a gesture of good will toward Iran in the context of negotiations over nuclear issues conducted in Europe.[66]

The Free Life Party ("PJAK")

PJAK is a militant Kurdish group operating out of Iraq. The group's leader is believed to be Abdul Rahman Hajji Ahmadi, a German citizen based in Germany. Many PJAK members are believed to be women who support the group's commitment to women's rights. This group has been formed in recent years and is known as the Iranian branch of PKK. The United States placed the PJAK on the U.S. FTO list in February 2009 because of the group's association with the Turkish Kurdish organization PKK, which has also been listed for some time.[67]

Convening Groups

Over the past years, efforts have been undertaken to bring the opposition groups together. These do not seem so far to have been very successful as the meetings have instead circled around flare-ups of personal and ideological rivalries. For example, a January 2004 meeting in Berlin ended, according to accounts, in argument over whether or not the restoration of monarchy should be an option.[68] For a meeting that took over a year to organize, the output was certainly a disappointment. There are a few problems to keep in mind with regard to these conferences. The intention is to encourage communication and build trust among the scattered opposition groups, but without proper care and a good agenda they can also just be occasions for an ongoing venting of long-standing animosities. They can then serve as unfortunate and demoralizing illus-

---

[65] See Moign Khawaja, "Iran Executes Jundullah Founder Abdul Malik Rigi," *Foreign Policy Journal*, June 20, 2010 <http://www.foreignpolicyjournal.com/2010/06/20/iran-executes-jundullah-founder-abdul-malik-rigi/>

[66] See Laura Rozen, "U.S. designates Jundullah as terrorist group," *Politico*, November 3, 2010 <http://www.politico.com/blogs/laurarozen/1110/US_designates_Jundullah_as_terrorist_group.html>

[67] See Katzman, "Iran: U.S. Concerns and Policy Responses," p. 17.

[68] See "Pro Republican Iranians Meet in Berlin," *Iran Press Service* <http://www.iran-press-service.com/articles_2004/Jan_04/iranian_republicans_meet_8104.htm>

trations of the weakness and division of the opposition. It is also important to be sure one knows who is convening and who is attending the gathering, and to what purpose. Iranian exiles relate instances of pseudo-meetings that were later found to have been choreographed by the Iranian regime.

At other times, opaque groupings may appear out of nowhere. An example is the Green Wave Movement, led by exiled London businessman Amir Jahanchahi, the son of the last Finance Minister under the Shah, and by Mehrdad Khonsari, a London-based Iranian academic. Jahanchahi announced that he would provide financial and logistical backing to any Iranian opposition groups, irrespective of their political ideologies, that were willing to move toward a common objective of regime change and democracy.[69] Jahanchahi claims to have established links with opposition civil society sectors in Iran, most notably with Mansour Osanloo, president of the Tehran bus workers' union *(Sharekat-e Vahed)*, a respected labor leader and human rights activist who Bernard-Henri Lévy calls the Iranian Lech Walesa, and members of the clergy in Qom and Tehran.[70] But the movement itself has no apparent organization associated with it, no record of activities, and thus the above claims are impossible to assess. In the midst of the uprising they organized a forum in France inviting other opposition members to join them. But it was revealed later that the group was infiltrated by the Iranian regime.[71]

Unaffiliated Intellectuals

The Internet has, as is well known, been critical as a vehicle for the ability of Iranian civil society to engage in political and social discourse and to maintain connections with the modern democratic outside world. The important players on this platform range from the "ordinary" bloggers to prominent, respected thought leaders inside and outside Iran. Some of the latter were formerly associated with a group or movement, and many were in jail at some point, but now are "unattached" Diaspora thinkers with followings of various size and composi-

---

[69] See "Launch of Green Wave Iran," <http://organization.greenwavenews.com/en/journal/303>

[70] See "Bernard-Henri Lévy on Mansour and Regime Change in Iran," The Middle East Online, March 6, 2013 <http://www.themiddleeastonline.com.au/?p=14918>

[71] See "Iran's Ministry of Intelligence and Security: A Profile, Federal Research Division," p. 30.

tion. As trusted voices, they are looked to for information and interpretation and have influence. In addition to their online presence, they typically also write for Iranian and Western newspapers and journals, are consulted by Western experts and governments, and are frequent guests at conferences and on panels. Examples would be persons such as Mehrangiz Kar, the human rights activist and lawyer now living in the U.S.; Abbas Milani, a scholar who is based at the Hoover Institution; Karim Sadjadpour who works with the Carnegie Endowment for International Peace. These persons do not consider themselves opposition figures; rather, they are dissident intellectuals and trusted information resources on Iranian affairs for Western think tanks and government agencies.

Unaffiliated Activists

Finally, and somewhat overlapping with the previous category, it is worth mentioning the large mass of unaffiliated activists who exist in the United States, Europe, as well as Turkey and other countries that have significant Iranian communities. These activists strongly dislike the regime, but for various reasons have elected not to affiliate with a particular opposition group.

The Green Movement

The term Green Movement is actually a misnomer. What became known as the Green Movement consisted of a series of events, some of them dramatic, but without a leadership or even a platform, and not constituting a movement. The political candidates who felt themselves to have been given short shrift in the 2009 election affiliated themselves with the wave of protests that followed, but they were more its symbols than its leaders. A wave of protest commenced after that election, manifesting in demonstrations and giving rise to the slogan "Where is my vote?" This catchy phrase along with information about the mass protests and photographs of the Basij and police cracking down with brutality on the demonstrators spread globally through social media. Opposition politicians emphasized their association with these events. For a brief period, it seemed as though Iran might be approaching a tipping point. The killing of a young student named Neda, captured on film and spread worldwide on You-Tube, was especially dramatic, but hers was not the only death caused by the regime's merciless repression. Many more were jailed, and allegations of torture and rape were widespread and persist to this day.

According to the Iranian League for the Defense of Human Rights, there were more than 100 verifiable deaths during the Green Movement protests and at least 2,000 opposition supporters were arrested. Mousavi and Karroubi were accused of sedition and are currently kept isolated and under guard; members of their family have also been victimized by the crackdown and episodically were jailed. Karroubi's political party, Etemad-e-Melli (National Confidence Party); the Mujahedeen of the Islamic Revolution party that supported Mousavi; and former President Khatami's IIPF have been banned, and opposition newspapers have been closed.[72] The center of gravity of the Green Movement was the students' movement at Tehran University and other universities across the country.[73] Currently, there is no organized student opposition. Dissenters at the universities are isolated, quickly identified by the Islamic Vigilance Committees, and expelled[74] or worse.[75]

The heightened expectations associated with the Green Movement were analogous to the hopes that earlier had been attached to the boom in civil society organizations or the blogger phenomenon. In all these instances, students and young people showed courage in expressing their opposition to the regime, and the dimensions and spread of the disaffect were startling.

While the Green Movement initially grew from a feeling of having been disenfranchised in the 2009 election, it quickly morphed into a broader critique of the Iranian regime. Indeed, as we noted, the slogan "Where is my vote?" soon changed to "Down with the principle of *velayat-e faqih*" and "Down with dicta-

---

[72] See Dieter Bednarz, "A Visit With Mahdi Karroubi: Iranian Opposition Leader Defiant Despite Government Crackdown," April 26, 2010, at http://www.spiegel.de/international/world/a-visit-with-mahdi-karroubi-iranian-opposition-leader-defiant-despite-government-crackdown-a-691198.html.

[73] See videos of demonstrations at Amirkabir University of Technology in Tehran, University of Hormozgan in southern Iran, and Ferdowsi University in Mashhad are available at "Iran students' day: Amateur videos," *BBC News*, December 7, 2009 <http://news.bbc.co.uk/2/hi/middle_east/8400244.stm>

[74] See Alain Chabod, "Universities, the heart of Iranian opposition," *France24*, March 1, 2010 <http://www.france24.com/en/20100101-2010-01-01-1843-week-middle-east-iran-opposition-universities>

[75] See Haleh Esfandiari, "Iran's State of Fear," *New York Review of Books*, March 3, 2011 <http://www.nybooks.com/blogs/nyrblog/2011/mar/03/irans-state-fear/>

tor." In that sense, the Green Movement outgrew even its own leadership as the main voices of the Green Movement, including Mussavi, Karroubi, Rafsanjani, and Khatami, all form part of the reformist camp which seeks to preserve the existing system of government while making some changes to it.

In the end, the will to resist was not sustainable in the face of the government's violent repression. As of today, the Green Movement is widely believed to have disbanded. While many of the students and other activists who took to the streets in 2009 still harbor the same levels of resentment against the regime, there is also a depressed sense within the country that the moment for change came and went, and that the regime won. In light of the scope and scale of the government's crackdown on the 2009 protestors, there is little desire to again put so much at risk for so little reward. The various elements of the Green Movement are a latent group of disaffected activists who, with the right leadership and a plausible vision, could be reactivated – but absent such leadership, it is highly unlikely that this group will again take matters into its own hands as it did in 2009.

Part III

Implications for U.S. Policy

5. Summary and Recommendations

The Islamic Revolution that overturned the Shah's regime caught the United States by surprise, and U.S. policy never really found its footing thereafter.

During the intervening decades, successive administrations have tried varying permutations of pressure, outreach, dialogue, negotiation, sanctions and threats, to no significant effect.

The victory of Hassan Rouhani in the June 2013 Iranian presidential elections is an example of the seemingly perplexing state of Iranian politics. Rouhani is a cleric with roots in the Islamic Revolution. He has played a central role in the development of Iran's nuclear program, particularly as chief nuclear negotiator from 2003 until 2005 and advocates for reducing international pressure on Iran. Rouhani has been hailed a moderate candidate, often referred to as 'the diplomat sheikh,' and he campaigned on platforms of pursuing constructive interaction with the West and easing economic sanctions, winning 50.7% of over 36 million votes cast in a country of 55 million eligible voters. But is Rouhani a reformer? Among 686 candidates who registered as presidential candidates, he was one of only eight allowed to run.[1] Rouhani is a pragmatist. He is a political insider, having served at the forefront of the Iran-Iraq war effort in the 1980s, a deputy speaker of parliament for years, and a member of the Assembly of Experts. He also spent 16 years as Secretary of the Supreme National Security Council. He remained Khamenei's representative in the Council until his election in June 2013. The short, medium, and long-term outcomes of his elections remain to be seen. Four scenarios are feasible:

1. Despite structural limitations on the presidency, Rouhani will attempt to bring about meaningful domestic reforms, including liberalization and economic developments while also seeking to constructively engage the West. Many U.S. experts remain hopeful that Rouhani's victory represents a fracturing of the Islamic state as an institution and can open up space for change. This scenario seems unlikely due to the Supreme Leader's power in determining the strategic principles of Iranian foreign policy.

2. Another possible outcome could be that Rouhani will make attempts to reform but will ultimately be stonewalled by the hard-liner elements and IRGC. There has been a prevailing narrative that the IRGC has "eclipsed" the clergy as an institution in terms of its internal political and economic influence and their management of the nuclear program.[2] Rouhani will have to contend with the more conservative blocs of Iranian politics, which could undermine his political position within the regime.

3. Rouhani could be intending to superficially pursue his campaign promises of engagement with the West in order to buy time to proceed with the country's nuclear strategy. Rouhani has made clear the importance of the Iranian nuclear program and has been seemingly disinclined to trade the nuclear program for other endeavors. It seems highly unlikely that Rouhani would have been permitted to run had his position threatened the Supreme Leader's agenda.

---

[1] See Alireza Nader, "Rouhani: Rival Constituencies," *United States Institute of Peace*, June 24, 2013 <http://iranprimer.usip.org/blog>
[2] See Sadjadpour, "Realistic Expectations for Iran's New President"

4. The possibility most hoped for by the West is that Rouhani genuinely stands behind his declared opening and has the standing and domestic support to deliver at least some significant initial change, upon which more can be built in the future.

It is critical to remember that successful diplomacy is interactive, not reactive. Too often, the debate even among analysts circles around the question of "what Iran intends" and "how should Rouhani be assessed." Those are relevant questions, but what happens will also depend on how the outside world responds. In the U.S., long-term advocates of engagement stress that the tentative rapprochement must be carefully nurtured. This is not wrong, but it is too simple. Rouhani is almost certainly testing the waters. If he is just pretending to be accommodating, and has no intention of truly following through, then the world must signal that it cannot be fooled, that it has ways and means of assessing Iran's intentions and conduct and will respond accordingly. Positive moves should be matched by positive responses, but Iran and Rouhani should not think that they are getting a free ride from a gullible world.

This means that there must be metrics and fact-based evaluations, but also that the West and the U.S. need a repertoire of nuanced responses and options, not just a pass-fail posture fueled by hope. The Iranian opposition can play a significant part in this.

- They can help by providing information about actual events inside Iran, including information about its nuclear program.

- They are a litmus test for whether or not the regime has any true reformist intentions.

- They can be a pressure point to let the Iranian regime know that if it does not make reasonable transformations, the world has alternative means of action.

- They can actively play a part in these transformations by competently utilizing any openings for democratic expression.

Economically, geo-strategically, and culturally, Iran is an important country with all the qualities to make it a leader in its region. But under the current religious autocracy, it has instead been playing a consistently negative international role. The decades-long inability of the U.S. to develop an effective foreign policy approach to the regime and its behavior is out of proportion to that importance and can have dangerous consequences in the near term. The Islamic regime equips and fosters terrorist groups. It is behind the current problems in Syria and Iraq. It ignores the will of the international community, does not honor its commitments and has been resistant to both carrots and sticks. Hopes for its eventual moderation through democratic processes have failed repeatedly, and it has managed to subdue the vehement popular protests and with them, the hopes for peaceful change. In defiance of the international community, it is on course to achieve nuclear weapons capability. This will not only magnify the risks associated with the aggressive behavior of the regime, but will cause multiple and cascading dangers in the region and is likely to spawn a nuclear arms race, taking the already dangerous sectarian strife to an unacceptable new level of risk.

6. Next Steps

A genuine solution will only occur once the regime in Iran is fundamentally transformed. There are two paths to such change. The first path assumes an Iranian glasnost with Rouhani in the role of Gorbachev. The second path becomes relevant if those expectations prove to be false, and foresees a radical internal change effected by an empowered and externally assisted Iranian opposition.

To increase the viability of both of these paths (or a combination of the two) there are a number of steps that the policy community and the U.S. government should consider:

- *Conduct deeper analysis of the rifts of the regime and of the opposition*

Developing a nuanced strategy requires a far more solid understanding than currently exists of both the internal rifts in the regime and of the opposition – the composition, the ideology and political platform, the size, and the capabilities of each group as well as their potential in a better environment. During the course of this project we were repeatedly struck by the dearth of solid data and information regarding these groups, and the high degree instead of assumptions, allegations and even gossip. Our study concentrated on filling this gap. Although we believe we have laid out an accurate initial picture of the opposition landscape, much more needs to be done. For a realistic assessment of all options, and for the USG to be able to make informed decisions about its policy course, this information is indispensable and should be pursued as thoroughly and speedily as possible.

Specifically, from the perspective of U.S. foreign policy, three questions are paramount when analyzing political opposition groups in countries where one is hoping to support change. These are:

1. Is this group fundamentally compatible with democratic values, human rights and peace in the region and the world? To the best of our knowledge, do we trust that their stated goals reflect their real intentions?[3]

2. Does this group possess capabilities to bring about change or play effective role in realizing change, and is the U.S. in a position to provide it with the assistance, advice, or backing it requires to take effective action?

- *Have a balanced approach to the regime and the opposition*

1. The opposition has never been a factor in the planning of the U.S. government, and this policy should be reviewed. Even during the Shah and despite having an enormous presence in Iran, the U.S. failed to recognize the trend of events and was therefore surprised by the revolution. An improved understanding and better reading of developments in the country requires strong communication with all sides, including the opposition.

2. This principally includes the MEK. This organization has very determined detractors inside the U.S. analytic and policy community, but many of their concerns were discovered to be unfounded during the

---

[3] It is of course possible for tactical reasons to support groups that are incompatible and even diametrically opposed to our values. However, historically, this has not typically been a successful approach for the U.S. and has frequently backfired, often with extremely dire and lasting consequences. We therefore decided to only consider groups who met the first criterion.

process of de-listing. The MEK is without a doubt the most active of Iran's opposition forces. To give this card away and to refuse this source of information without cause is irresponsible.

- *View the opposition additively – not necessarily as alternatives or even as a coalition*

In studying previous instances of attempted system change through backing an opposition to an autocratic regime, we can distinguish several different approaches.

1. Diffuse support to alternative values and to civil society, typically through media campaigns and through funding of dissidents and civil society groups and lending platforms to the rival ideology. This was widely done during the Cold War.

2. Ideological, financial and/or military support to groups launching an uprising against a dictator or hostile regime. If this uprising was unexpected, there is often insufficient time to obtain good information about the rebels and their platforms and affiliations. This can become a serious problem later.

3. Ideological, financial and/or military support to selected groups who are deemed for various reasons to be most suitable. These reasons include ideological affinity, but the decision can also be mainly tactical. During the Soviet occupation of Afghanistan, for example, the U.S. threw its support behind extremist Islamist groups, partly because they were guided by Pakistan in this decision, and partly because it was thought that these groups would fight the hardest and thus would impose the highest costs on the Soviets. They were not expected to win, so their ideology was not thought to matter. Obviously, this was a mistake with enormous consequences.

4. More recently, U.S. policy has shown a preference for supporting consortiums of opposition groups, i.e., "bringing together" the opposition. This was attempted in Libya and is presently still being attempted for Syria. Gatherings are convened in which the various opposition groups are supposed to agree on a joint platform and ideally a shared leadership.

These can be time-consuming and largely futile exercises, with opportunism rather than genuine will motivating otherwise hostile groups to participate without affecting their intention to resume their rivalries as soon as the convening outside power has left the room.

For Iran, we propose consideration of a different approach, in which the opposition is viewed additively. Instead of expending effort on forcing a coalition, in this approach the groups would instead be assessed for their particular strengths and for the role that they can best play during different stages of a regime change operation. On the basis of such choreography, they would then be invited to join forces for a clearly defined purpose. In the case of Iran, the most important first step is to enter into dialogue with the opposition. So far as the different U.S. administrations are concerned, the bulk of the Iranian opposition has been operating in a hostile environment, thus seriously constraining their abilities and needlessly self-limiting U.S. policy options at a time when maximum leverage should be sought.

We believe engaging the Iranian opposition – and in this additive way – is advisable for three reasons:

1. It is the appropriate counter-measure to one of the regime's most effective tactics, that of criminalizing its opponents.

2. The resources, abilities and liabilities of the groups are different and potentially complementary. Indeed, this stands in contrast to some other countries where opposition groups have very few or have redundant capabilities. The Iranian resistance when taken in sum delivers a complementary range of resources and competencies, which with support could be considerably amplified.

3. While complicated personal histories and rivalries may make it difficult for many of these groups and their leaders and members to suddenly become friends and allies, objectively there is considerable overlap in their aims. They may have started out from starkly divergent ideological positions during the 1970s, but today they are in agreement regarding the desirable outcome for Iran[4] – a secular/laicist democracy in which all parties can contend.

---

[4] It is obvious that a stated purpose cannot be taken at face value, but as we will explain, opportunities to hijack a revolution will be far slimmer in this instance than they were in Arab Spring or at the time of the overthrow of the Shah.

- *Establish a process for liaising with the opposition*

The United States should rescind its current policy of not dealing directly with Iranian opposition groups. This policy undermines the U.S. ability to get to know, convene and otherwise work with the exact groups we should be interacting closely with right now. The information they can provide should be considered and assessed and relationships built.

The U.S. already has personnel based in Dubai and London that monitor developments in Iran. Expanding their remit or adding additional staff to liaise with opposition groups would not be particularly resource-intensive.

- *Engage the MEK*

The MEK is by far the largest and strongest of the opposition groups. It has a proven record of resiliency and ideological consistency over time. As soon as Khomeini's intentions became obvious, it declared its opposition to a theocratic state, and that remains its view.

The group has strong organizational skills, group cohesiveness and penetration of Iranian regime institutions that allow it to collect sensitive intelligence. The Iranian regime considers it to represent the principal threat to its continued rule, as evidenced by a robust propaganda machinery dedicated to its denunciation, and by the ongoing arrests, imprisonment, and executions of its members and sympathizers. The regime has expended considerable and persistent energy on an international campaign to hound this group out of its various places of exile, for example, by striking under-the-table deals in which European hostages were released to their governments in exchange for the eviction of MEK officials who previously had de facto asylum; and in propaganda campaigns to portray them as a sinister cult. On repeated occasions, alleged victims of MEK cult persecution have been exposed as agents of Iranian intelligence, but the Iranian regime has been able to exploit the general inattentiveness to detail and lack of due diligence on the part of Western Iran observers to affix the cult label. As the most effective opposition group, they are also the most powerful potential card for the West to play, and forfeiting it makes no sense.

- *Support Opposition Media and Social Networks*

The U.S. should generally support opposition media and social networking platforms to keep up pressure.

Iranian opposition groups based abroad rely on a variety of media and social networks to influence Iranian audiences, including broadcasting, the Internet, Facebook, Twitter, YouTube, Flickr, and text messaging. Taken in sum, this has successfully stymied the Iranian regime's efforts to control the information flow.

The pro-MEK 24-hour Simile Azadi or Iran National Television ("INTV"), which is banned in Iran, broadcasts news and information to Iranians all around the world via satellite and the Internet. The MEK also operate several websites in Farsi as well as in English, French, Arabic, German and Italian.

The deputy chief of the Iranian regime's television broadcast operation admitted in 2010 that despite the ban, 40% of Iranian homes have access to satellite television. Due to increased Internet censorship and surveillance that has led to the tracking down and arrest of many online activists inside Iran, many have turned to this network as a way to obtain real information without being traced.[5] The network also includes entertainment content such as satirical programs, children's programs, and some call-in shows that offer glimpses into popular attitudes in the country.

Jonesy Raphe Sabs,[6] known as Jars[7], is a Persian-language online news site established in June 2009 by a group of dissident Iranian politicians and journalists, mostly living in the United States and Europe, as a platform for stories about events in Iran. Jars is on YouTube and plans to introduce an Internet TV channel and satellite TV. The site has a moderate religious viewpoint and three of its board members supported Moussa's platform for the Green Movement in 2009. This website pursues reform in the *velayat-e faqih* system and not regime change. The Jars staff accepts only private donations.[8]

---

[5] See Abbas Rezai, "Iranian Opposition TV Gets Record Backing," *Huffington Post*, January 31, 2013, at http://www.huffingtonpost.co.uk/abbas-rezai/iranian-opposition-tv-gets-record-backing_b_2586486.html.

[6] See Jaras Website <http://www.rahesabz.net/>

[7] Spelling variations for Jars and Simile Azadi exist. Spellings used here were provided by our Iranian consultant.

[8] See "From Outside Iran Jaras Reports on the Green Movement," European Journalism Centre, January 25, 2010 http://www.ejc.net/magazine/article/from_outside_iran_jaras_reports_on_the_Green_Movement/

RoozOnline is a Persian and English language news website published by the Iran Gooya media group, which is registered in France. RoozOnline is funded by Hivos, a Dutch non-governmental organization that works with Iranian civil society organizations and receives funding from the Dutch government.[9] In 2010 the Iranian Intelligence Ministry published a list of organizations including Hivos that it accused of promoting 'soft regime change' in Iran.[10]

Conclusion

The U.S. should follow a multi-faceted, judicious policy that encourages steady improvement in U.S.-Iranian relations if possible, but remains grounded in reality, one that carefully assesses and monitors actual Iranian regime conduct, taking also into account the critical area of human rights, one seduced neither by unfounded hopes nor by the impatience of Western business interests to finally be allowed access to the resources of that country. Further, given how consequential a misjudgment could be, the U.S. must assure that it has a range of options for the event that Iranian politicians are dissimulating. Principal among these options is to build and sustain a relationship with the Iranian opposition.

Empowering the Iranian opposition is a key policy tool the U.S. has ignored for too long. Washington must immediately embark upon developing an understanding of who the groups are, what they stand for, and what capabilities they have or could acquire, and then begin to reach out to them. Such an approach acknowledges the reality that the opposition can improve the prospects for bringing about an Iran that does not pose a threat to global stability or to its own people. The sooner Washington embraces the policy, the sooner U.S.-Iranian relations can begin to improve.

---

[9] See RoozOnline Website <http://www.roozonline.com/english/>
[10] "Hivos Has Never Promoted Regime Change," April 10, 2010, at http://www.roozonline.com/english/news3/newsitem/article/hivos-has-never-promoted-regime-change.html.

U.S. Sanctions	UN Sanctions	EU Sanctions
Ban on U.S. trade and investment in Iran (Executive Order 12959) • Limited exceptions, including for food and medical exports	No restrictions on civilian trade with Iran.	No general ban on trade in civilian goods, but oil embargo and banking sanctions together have similar impact.
Sanctions on foreign companies that do business with Iran's energy sector (Iran Sanctions Act) • Sanction nearly all transactions • Limited exemptions for countries that "significantly reduce" purchases of Iranian oil	No equivalent	EU measures from July 27, 2010 ban grants, aid, and loans to Iran, in addition to financing of companies involved in Iran's energy sector.
Ban on arms exports • No U.S. arms can be sold to Iran under several laws	UN Member States banned from selling or supplying major weapons systems to Iran (UNSC Resolution 1929)	EU sanctions ban sales of all types of military equipment to Iran (not just major weapons systems).
Restrictions on export of dual-use items • All licenses must be denied for sale of any dual-use item that could have a military purpose (Export Administration Act; Arms Exports Control Act)	Several UNSC resolutions together ban most dual-use items, too.	EU abides by UN restrictions; Oct 2012 EU sanctions ban graphite and finished metal sales to Iran.
Sanctions against foreign firms that sell WMD-related technology to Iran • Numerous sanctions in various laws to absolutely ban this practice	Worldwide freeze on assets and properties of Iranian entities named as subject to sanctions (UNSC Re. 1737).	EU honors UN resolutions per July 27, 2010 EU measures.

Appendix

U.S. Sanctions	UN Sanctions	EU Sanctions
Ban on transactions with terrorism-supporting entities (Executive Order 13224) • Numerous entities designated under this order	No direct equivalent; ban on Iran exporting any arms (e.g., to Hezbollah) (UNSC Res. 1747).	No direct equivalent, but many of the entities named by the U.S. overlap with E.U. blocked entities.
Travel ban on named Iranians • No travel to U.S., transfer of U.S. property, or any transactions with individuals involved in serious human rights abuses in Iran since 2009, the 2009 presidential election, etc.	Binding travel ban on Iranian named in UNSC Res. 1803; Extended to 40 individuals via UNSC Res. 1929. Involvement in nuclear weapons program, not human rights abuses determines the ban.	EU sanctions from July 2010 named Iranians subject to a travel ban; expanded to include human rights offenders.
Restrictions on shipping • Islamic Republic of Iran Shipping Lines (IRISL) and affiliated entities with U.S. property frozen (Executive Order 13382)	Member States may inspect and seize cargoes carried by IRISL – or any ships in national or international waters – if there is a belief that shipment include banned goods destined for Iran (UNSC Res. 1803 and 1929).	EU sanctions from July 2010 ban Iran Air Cargo access to EU airports; assets of IRISL in Europe frozen; and insurance and re-insurance for Iranian shipping firms banned.
Banking Sanctions • All banking relationships with U.S. banks or any foreign bank that conducts transactions with IRGC or any UN-sanctioned Iranian entity banned • No U.S. accounts allowed in foreign banks that process transactions with Iran's Central Bank	No direct equivalent; two Iranian banks are sanctioned entities under UNSC resolutions.	Extensive banking sanctions • Iranian Central Bank assets in EU frozen and all transactions with Iranian banked banned • Brussels-based SWIFT expels sanctioned Iranian banks from electronic payment transfer system • UK banned any transactions with Iranian Central Bank

About METIS Analytics

METIS is a Washington, DC-based research company that conducts studies on strategic and political issues and advises on issues related to human rights and post-conflict transitions.

Authors: Cheryl Benard, Austin Long, Angel Rabasa, Eli Sugarman

Acknowledgements

We wish to acknowledge some foundational research conducted by Alexander Benard on think tank positions vis-á-vis Iran; by Azadeh Pourzand on Iranian blogging; by Marri Janeka on the Iranian connection of radical groups; and by Sophia Schultz on the independent Iranian artist scene. We are grateful to the many colleagues and activist individuals who provided information and guidance; they are too numerous or, in the case of some Iranian colleagues, too politically vulnerable to name. The U.S. Department of State Iran Watch offices in Dubai and London provided their insights, for which we thank them. Special appreciation must go to our editor, Phil Hanrahan, for shepherding this project expeditiously and caringly to its timely conclusion.

CPSIA information can be obtained at www.ICGtesting.com
Printed in the USA
BVOW03s0937190515

400879BV00004B/31/P

9 780692 399378